The Simple Guide to Selling Your
Dental Practice for More Money

The Simple Guide to Selling Your Dental Practice For More Money

By Manfred Purtzki, CPA, CA

Blue Beetle Books

First published 2021
Trade paperback ISBN: 978-1-7778287-0-7

Blue Beetle Books Inc., Victoria, B.C.
www.bluebeetlebooks.com
Tel: 250.704.6686

Inquiries regarding requests to reprint all or part of *The Simple Guide to
Selling Your Dental Practice for More Money* should be addressed to Manfred
Purtzki at the address below.

Purtzki Transitions Inc.
1700-570 Granville Street
Vancouver, BC
V6C 3P1
Tel: 778-288-2920
Email: manfred@purtzki.com

It is recommended that legal, accounting, and other professional advice
is sought before acting on any information contained in this book as each
individual's financial circumstances are unique.

Written in collaboration with Mike Wicks.
Cover design and book layout by Tom Spetter.
Custom publishing services provided by Blue Beetle Books Inc.

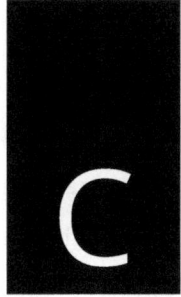

C

Contents

P

Preface

Let's get one thing straight from the outset—the primary objective of this book is to help you sell your practice, whenever you are ready, for more money than you ever thought possible. Other than perhaps your house and assuming you are successful, your practice is your most significant asset. Unlocking that potential at the right time and in the right way, can mean the difference between an okay retirement, and one that is everything you ever dreamed it might be. *The Simple Guide to Selling Your Dental Practice for More Money* is full of practical advice, and enough horror stories to make you sit up and pay attention. Make no mistake, it's not that difficult to screw up and be left with nothing—literally nothing. The true story about Dr. Kristy, in chapter eight, is testimony to that statement.

Hopefully I have your attention now. Sorry about the scare tactics, but sometimes it's necessary. Don't worry, I've got your back. All you need to do is take a few precautions, plan ahead, and you'll do well. And hey, I'm here to guide you through every step of the transition process to ensure you maximize your sale proceeds when the time comes.

Experts say that the time to start planning your exit is when you write your practice start-up business plan. If your practice has already been around for a while, don't panic, it's never too late to start planning the sale of your practice. Once you've made that commitment, you will grow your practice with a focus on both the business, and patient-care sides. You will find yourself making decisions that make your practice more efficient—and hence, more profitable. Your end goal should be to optimize the long-term value of your practice.

For the past forty years I have advised and worked with dentists in a number of different capacities. When I launched my accounting firm in 1980, my dentist—and first dental practice client—Dr. Fern Savoie, suggested that I make a few presentations to his local study group as a way to build my clientele. As a result of presenting to the group and referrals from Fern, who was very well-connected, I brought in several new clients.

Those early days were tough. I had a wife and three children, and those early dentist clients helped me become established. Things went well until later that year, when the economy went into free fall, prime spiked to 16% and unemployment in many industry sectors hit 25%. Even healthy companies went under or were on life support. It lasted for two years. The funny thing was, dentists seemed almost immune; it was like they were recession proof. Clinics remained busy and dentists enjoyed a steady income, unlike my other business clients, many of whom were struggling. It's a not-so-funny fact that accountants put their expense as the first item on the income statement but are usually the last to be paid. It was against this background that I decided to focus on servicing dental practices and retired most of my small business clients.

Over the past forty years I have loved every minute of my time working with dentists. At the beginning, I provided the usual CPA services of accounting and income tax. At times I was both the clinic bookkeeper and Chief Financial Officer. I looked after banking and arranged loans. I helped dentists with their personal financial planning. On many occasions, I saved a dentist from losing their retirement nest egg by preventing them from signing up for leaky (read, *shady*) tax shelters. I'd even assist with the termination of employees for the less-business-savvy, good-hearted dentists. My dental clinic clients grew in both size and number, and I began helping them bring on new associates. When the time came for an associate to buy into a clinic and become a partner, I was there to handle implementation. I learned a lot over the years about managing, selling, and buying dental practices by being in the trenches with my dentist clients on a daily basis.

However, it wasn't long before I realized that while dentists never needed to worry about generating sufficient income to lead a good life, many needed the proceeds from the sale of their practice to supplement their retirement portfolio. When the time came to sell, my clients turned to me to help them with practice valuations and the hundred-and-one other things that muddy the waters during a dental transition. I enjoyed working with dentists, especially in exceeding their expectations when it came to the final selling price of their practices. Gradually, practice transitions took up more of my time, so a few years ago I transitioned my CPA firm to a very capable successor. This allowed me to concentrate on my passion; guiding dentists through the most important financial milestones in their career, buying or selling a practice, or even starting a clinic from scratch. Unlike accounting and tax, which are annual events, brokering a dental clinic is a transactional event, so I continually meet new people and face new challenges. My favorite thing of all, though, is creating long-lasting relationships with my clients.

As far as my clients are concerned, my goal is always to be useful, add value, and always be their trusted advisor. This book is an extension of that promise; please make use of the advice it contains and if you need any help, please feel free to reach out to me at manfred@purtzki.com and I'll be happy to answer any questions you might have.

Manfred Purtzki (www.purtzkitransitions.com)

The Simple Guide to Selling Your Dental Practice For More Money

CHAPTER

1

Thinking of Selling Your Practice?

Have you ever thought about selling your practice? I don't mean right now, but sometime in the future. No? Then you should. I know, I know—you are run off your feet looking after patients, managing staff, and the hundred and one other things you must do every day to keep the revenue flowing. You have responsibilities. Thinking about retirement, transitioning to a new career, moving to a Caribbean Island and buying a fishing charter boat, writing that novel—all those things can wait, right? Well, yes and no.

It is never too early to plan for the future. Practice transition experts advise that the best time to start planning to sell your practice, is the day you start the practice. That may be somewhat of an exaggeration, but the sound advice behind the hyperbole is that the more advance planning you do and the more systems you put in place, the better prepared you'll be when the time does come to step down. More importantly, you will make more money when you eventually sell.

Take a few minutes to think about what you have built. If you are like most dentists, dentistry has been your all-consuming passion ever since you graduated from high school, went to college, racked up a ton of debt in student loans (thankfully paid off years ago), practiced as an associate, and finally built your own practice. A practice which is now successful, respected by your peers, admired by your staff, and loved by your patients. However, at the back of your mind is that niggling thought—what is my exit strategy? What have I worked for all these years? When do I begin to reap the rewards of all my hard work?

If you are younger this may seem to be some years off, although in today's fast-changing world increasing numbers of professionals are looking to the excitement and challenge of a second career. Innovation, and the crazy pace of social, cultural, and technological change, not to mention increasing longevity (70 really will be the new 50), are presenting new and exciting opportunities every day.

Maybe it's simply time for a second career or like any successful Broadway show, time for the final curtain. You may have been mentally preparing for this final day for years—looking forward to writing a new script for your life after dentistry, liberated from the daily grind, ready to enjoy your new-found freedom.

Wherever you are on the spectrum, even if you are not yet ready to hang up the "for sale" sign, you would be wise to think about the steps you will need to take today or tomorrow, to exit your practice. When the time comes, you have one chance to execute the sale perfectly and maximize the return on your investment. Advance preparation is key; don't leave transition planning to the eve of your retirement, by then it will be too late and I guarantee you will leave a ton of money on the table.

Paul Simon said, "There are fifty ways to leave your lover." Well, that's also true about leaving your practice, so let me give you the wealth of my almost forty years of experience of how to exit your practice with more money than you ever thought possible.

Ensure You Are Emotionally Ready to Sell Your Practice

Leaving your practice behind, handing over your life's work, your staff, and your patients to someone else is a major decision—practically, as well as emotionally. Regardless of whether you are keen to sell and have big plans for your post-dental career, or you are looking forward to a new life in retirement, I suggest you take a few moments to reflect on what it really means. Imagine your life if you were to simply walk away from your practice and from dentistry. Ask yourself how much of your identity is wrapped up in your profession—in being a dentist.

They say old habits die hard. Think about how long you have owned the practice. How many years have you risen early five or six days a week anticipating the morning huddle with your team? Long-time staff members respect you as a leader, many have become friends. Loyal patients trust you with their well-being, and many look forward to their appointments. Some, also, have become friends.

Over the years, you have spent countless hours honing your skills through professional development courses to stay at the top of your game. Perhaps your philosophy has been, "Do what's best for the patient and the money will follow," and that has helped you build a practice that has exceeded your expectations. Maybe, work has been all-consuming and there has been little time for anything else, including hobbies.

What will happen once you leave the practice completely and hand the keys to your successor? Retirement? Will that be a blessing or a curse? Some people experience the thrill of freedom while others feel adrift and lack motivation. Think carefully about what life will look like when you don't have your practice. I have witnessed the emotional toll retirement exacts on many of my clients who retire and then struggle to find a new purpose in life.

The more passionate you are about dentistry, the harder it will be to let go and start a new life. Many practice sales are aborted at the last minute, not because of buyer's remorse surrounding the deal, but because the seller was not able to give up practicing as a dentist. Of course, the reverse is true for those who have a less emotional attachment to dentistry and enjoy a full and active life apart from their practice. If you view the transition as a financial transaction, not an emotional event, things will go a lot smoother.

I am often asked, "How do I know when I'm ready to quit?" Usually by someone who is weighing the pros and cons of continuing to work or selling the practice and playing golf every day. Strangely, I get asked this most often on fine spring and summer days. I suggest they use the mirror test. Try it yourself—when you first look at yourself in the mirror each morning ask yourself, "If I had only a few days left on this earth, would I go to my practice today?" If for five mornings in a row you answer in the negative, you are probably ready to transition into retirement or a new career without looking back with regret.

Don't Make Spur-of-the-Moment Decisions

One trap that is easy to fall into is to accept an unsolicited offer. Here's the scenario: a dentist, or their agent, approaches you with an offer to purchase your practice out of the blue. "Wow, you think, that's cool!" It seems like a lot of money and it's so easy. You begin to dream of all the things you could do with your free time and all that money. Stop! The only thing you should do with that offer is reject it. That may seem harsh but hear me out. There are two reasons; first, you will almost certainly get more money if you put your practice on the open market. Second, in almost all cases an unsolicited offer will rarely coincide with your carefully planned transition. Which is, of course, another reason to have a well thought out transition plan in the first place—just in case. So, here's what I suggest you do when that crazy offer arrives, listen carefully: lie down on a couch (or even your dental chair), take two aspirins, and wait until the urge to sell goes away.

Take Stan, a sixty-five-year-old dentist client of mine. Over the years his practice has generated a lot of income; unfortunately, he is still struggling to pay down his mortgage. Not least because he has never learned to say "No" to his two adult children and continues to finance their overly lavish lifestyle. Over the last few years, the sharks have been circling his practice which is in a desirable seaside community. He has frequently received unsolicited offers which he has always resisted. But, like the waves eroding the cliffs along the beach close to his practice, and unbeknownst to me, he started to warm to the idea despite his poor financial situation. In light of this, I was not surprised to get a call from him one bright spring morning recently, telling me that he had accepted an offer for his practice. My accountant's heart sunk. His rationale was that the large chunk of money would help him pay off the mortgage. Unfortunately, this would be at the cost of saving for his retirement. A bad day, or few days, can result in a knee-jerk decision that doesn't take into consideration your long-term financial needs.

Another client, Janie, began to hate going to work. Two of her staff members had destroyed office morale with their constant bickering and complaining. The poor atmosphere was being felt by patients, and Janie became despondent. She could have chosen to buckle down and clean house; fire the troublemakers and bring order to her practice. However, she took the first out-of-the-blue offer that turned up and sold the high-grossing practice she had owned for fifteen years. The buyer was keen, and contracts were signed just a few weeks later. Seller's remorse kicked in shortly after. Janie never thought things through; she had no plan unless it was to escape at any cost. Subsequently, she worked as an associate in another office for a while before buying a small practice. She never felt fulfilled though. She felt she had failed to reach her potential, and her earnings fell far short of what they had been in her old clinic. In Janie's case a spur of the moment decision destroyed her career, and maybe her life.

Don't Make Money the Most Important Consideration

Here's a trick question: you put your practice on the market several months ago and now have two firm offers, one for $750,000 and one for $800,000—which one do you choose? Okay, I'm not being fair because I'm asking the wrong question. A better question is: you have two offers, which one is better? Even that question is a little tricky to answer because it all depends on what type of dentist you are, what type of person you are, how you run your practice, and how well you want to sleep at night in retirement.

If you are considering selling your practice you first need to know whether you are willing to sell your soul to the God of mammon. How important is making the most money compared to finding a successor with a compatible practice philosophy to yours? Have you spent your career taking time with each patient, never rushing treatment, taking the conservative, caring approach? Will you put a suspect tooth on a watchlist, rather than pushing for immediate treatment to maximize profit? If that sounds familiar, then you and your practice have almost certainly earned the trust of your patients. You know this because when you propose a treatment plan, patients overwhelmingly accept it. There is great value in that and we're not talking about just money.

The bottom line is that it's good karma to sell your practice to a dentist with a similar practice philosophy. How important is your legacy? Is it important enough to leave it in good hands? The last thing you want is to make a few extra thousand dollars and leave your patients in the hands of a dentist who puts their needs ahead of your patients. Goodwill is hard to build and easy to lose. Sell to the wrong successor and you will be in danger of running into your old patients on the street, complaining that you abandoned them.

There are many ways to ensure you get the right fit; my tip is never leave it to your advisors and do your own due diligence on prospective purchasers. Remember, it is your legacy and your reputation. It took hard work and integrity to build a career—don't let a stranger destroy it.

Involve Your Partner in the Transition

You may rule the roost in your practice and make all the tough decisions, but don't fall into the trap of thinking you can make the decision to sell your practice, or transition to fewer days a week, without talking it over with your spouse. Retirement, and even semi-retirement, is a transition on the home front as well as at the office. Almost everyone dreams of retirement: time to travel, garden, golf. It all seems like an earthly paradise, but in reality—not so much.

I saw how wrong an unplanned retirement can go when Richard, a long-time client of mine, decided to cut back his hours with little to no prior discussion with his wife. She had retired a few years previously and had developed daily routines; she met regularly with friends, volunteered, and had many hobbies. The trouble started when Richard began working a four-day week. He quickly discovered that he had no real hobbies, so he thought it would be nice to "hang out" with his wife. This "loving" gesture was not appreciated, and she immediately found him too clingy. The last straw was when she was shopping at Costco with friends and turned to find Richard following them a few paces behind. Poor Richard was lost, and that was just one day a week. Right there and then, in the middle of the store, she ordered him back to his office. Wisely, and a little sheepishly, he did as he was told. She confided in me shortly after that she dreads the day he fully retires.

To avoid this type of conflict, talk to your spouse about the transition. The more opportunity you both have to air your concerns, the better the chance you will have to build a mutually agreeable plan. Make the transition of your practice a frequent topic at the dinner table; it's easy to find love and common ground over a glass of wine and a good steak.

Make Sure You Can Afford to Retire

It sounds a little obvious, but take it from me, you'll need more than you think—maybe a lot more. I talked earlier about the need to plan your sale well in advance, well, here is a reason to do it even decades before it becomes a reality—saving for retirement takes time. That nest egg matures slowly, and it needs to last you a lifetime. And a lot will depend on the level of luxury you want your "lifetime" to include. An annual world cruise doesn't come cheap. My advice is to only sell when you have enough money to lead the life you want to live for the rest of your life.

For example, consider Mike and Tammy's situation. Mike is turning sixty-five this year and is ready to sell his practice. Recently, the couple asked a financial planner to work out a plan to provide an income projection for their retirement based on their expected $2 million in retirement savings. This included a projected $700,000 from the sale of the practice. They own a home, mortgage free. The financial planner projected that the retirement nest egg would yield $70,000 per year before tax for the rest of their lives. While the $70,000 per year would take care of their basic needs, it does not allow for much else.

Of course, what would have been a heck of a lot better was if they had planned for retirement shortly after they opened their dental practice. Unfortunately, that ship had sailed for them. Take note if you are just starting out—retirement has a habit of creeping up on you.

Find the Right Transition Model for Your Circumstances

I'll be discussing the various transition models in a lot more detail in chapter four, for now just be aware of your options and consider which one might work for you. Bear in mind, a lot will depend on the timing of your sale.

- *The Complete Sale*—This is the straightforward retirement sale.
- *The Delayed Complete Sale*—A variation of the complete sale.
- *Solo Group*—In this model you sell a fractional interest in the practice.
- *Partnership*—an alternative to solo group which is gaining in popularity.
- *Merger of Practices*— Merging with another practice which occupies a larger space.
- *Sale to a Dental Service Organization (DSO)*

Okay, are you prepared? Are you excited about selling and moving on to the next stage of your life, or transitioning your practice in preparation for selling at a later date? Well, there's a lot to do if you want to maximize your sale price, walk out the door, wave goodbye to your faithful staff, and get into that well-deserved Maserati Quattroporte. And it all begins with preparing your practice for sale.

2

Maximize Selling Price

Understand the Value of Your Practice

If you can wave a magic wand to increase the net income of your practice by $100,000, how much more can you expect on a practice sale? $200,000 or $300,000? Would you believe that you can potentially get $500,000 or more by increasing your net income by just $100,000? That boost would put your retirement nest egg on steroids. Bora Bora, here I come.

Let me bring you down to earth a little and explain why this is possible. Purchasers today are less likely to use the old way of valuing your practice, which was to base it on a percentage of gross revenues. And they are wise to do so because gross revenues don't tell the whole story. Dentists looking to purchase a practice are thinking like investors, they are focused on ROI (Return of Investment). Their focus is on the net operating income (some people call this cash flow). Basically, it's all about the bottom line—you know, profit. The trendy new acronym is EBITDA (Earnings Before Interest, Taxes, Depreciation, and Amortization). Now, don't get nervous, this isn't as complicated or frightening as it might first appear. EBITDA has been around for years, but it's mostly been the purview of people acquiring real estate and businesses. These people used EBITDA because when they purchased income-producing real estate they were less interested in the property itself, but the income it produced. In effect, they were purchasing cash flow. And that's how they valued the property.

Let's take a scenario where Penny Profit is considering a purchase. She is looking for a 5% return on her investment and the property she has in mind generates an annual net income of $100,000. In this case she would be prepared to pay $2 million (*Quick Math–$100,000/5%*).

Now here's the thing, you have an income-producing business. It may be specialized, but the same principles apply to selling your practice as selling a real estate income property.

A lot changed when corporations entered the dental market and started acquiring dental clinics. For a start, they used the EBITDA formula to determine the purchase price. As a result, this formula is now widely used in practice acquisitions.

Let's circle back to my magic wand promise. If you increase the operating cash flow, or EBITDA, by a mere $100,000, the value of your practice will grow by $500,000 at a cap rate of 20%. It really pays to focus on revenue when trying to maximize sale proceeds.

Increasing the net income can be achieved in several ways, one of which is to trim expenses. If you can make your practice a little leaner, perhaps by cross-training your staff to assume multiple roles and reducing dental supply costs and other office expenses, your profits will naturally head north. Of course, spending time trying to save a few dollars here and there is often less productive than building revenues, so you really need to focus on increasing the office production.

I can hear you saying, "but where do I start?" Counter-intuitively, my advice is not to jump straight in to developing strategies to increase your net income. I know, you are keen to get going and you want to start bringing in money, but as I mentioned earlier, a little planning goes a long way.

The first step is to ensure you have an accounting system in place that will produce detailed financial statements within days of each month-end. In my experience, many dental practices simply don't have access to the information they need to make informed decisions. As Oscar Wilde said, "If you don't know where you are going, any road will take you there."

Many practice owners are so involved in day-to-day dentistry that they have little idea about the financial health of their practice. Until, of course, their accountant sends them the annual income statement. Some dentists are only concerned about the amount of money if the bank line of credit is getting close to the maximum.

Maintaining solid management information systems will provide everyone involved with your practice transition the information they need to assist and guide you to realizing the best price for your practice.

Increase Revenues—Don't Slow Down Just Because You Are Selling

Buyers will not care how much revenue you made over the past fifteen years. They, and their advisors, will focus on your last few years' gross revenue, net profit, and positive cash flow. More importantly, they will show special interest in the practice's current year. What matters most is how your practice has performed recently. A trend showing declining revenues will have potential purchasers running to the next practice on their list, or they will try to mercilessly beat you down to get a bargain-basement deal. Excellent, supported predictions of financial viability and sustainability are key parameters used by savvy purchasers to identify prime practices. The golden rule is: never let your revenues decline. As you transition from thinking about selling to doing something about it, it can be tempting to slow down or work fewer days. Don't!

Increasing practice revenues can be achieved in several ways. One way is to compare your fees to that of your competitors and the industry standard. If they are on the low side, bump them up a little. This tactic can be an easy way to increase the value of your practice without having to work harder. There is a tendency as dentists get older and more financially secure to become less aggressive in annually raising their fees. When did you last increase your fees?

We live in competitive times so bringing in new patients is not always easy. If you are well-established, then chances are you may not even have a website or actively use social media. Many highly successful practices are living in the golden glow of the past. If you want to sell, however, that must change. You will need to bring your practice into the 21st century.

I know many dentists who are social media savvy but who tell me their marketing efforts have only helped with patient attrition, and that their patient numbers remain steady, but any increase is moderate at best. Often this is because they confuse marketing with selling. In fact, the two words are often— erroneously—used interchangeably. The reality is that marketing raises awareness and produces inquiries, but someone must convert that interest into signed-up patients. That is, somebody must bring new patients through the door. That person is usually your receptionist. Let me hold your feet to the fire for a second; does your front-desk person have the skills to sell someone on your practice? Honestly? When a prospect calls, do they know how to turn that incoming call into a practice visit? And it's not just the front-desk; selling is the job of every member of staff. It involves direct contact either over the phone, face-to-face in the clinic, or these days via videoconferencing. Marketing without selling is trying to bail out a boat with a hole in it. Only the act of selling will boost patient count, and that in turn is what will increase the value of your practice when the time comes to sell.

There are many programs to assist in your staff training. One of note is the Ritz-Carlton program. Ritz-Carlton is famous for its legendary culture of outstanding customer service. To create a high-level "culture of service," you will also need to have frequent motivational employee sessions that emphasize customer service. Why would using the Ritz-Carlton approach, or something similar, help make your practice successful? The level of customer care that it promotes gives patients a sense of belonging; it makes them feel that they are somebody special. Every time a patient pays his or her bill and leaves the practice, even when that bill is a shock, you want them to think, "That was a good experience, and I got value for money." Combining first-class customer service with outstanding clinical care has immense potential to boost new patient referrals and case acceptance.

In chapter 3, I will give you further strategies to help you maximize cash flow and therefore the value of your practice.

Reduce Overhead as a Percentage of Gross Revenues

High overheads are one of the biggest stumbling blocks to selling a practice. There are many clinics on the market that are generating less net income than an average associate earns.

Why then would a dentist be interested in taking the financial risks involved in buying such a practice? They could have the same level of earnings without the headaches that come with managing a practice. This is the reason it's tough to sell a practice that is not being run cost-effectively.

However, it is a relatively simple fix. Increasing the practice's revenues automatically decreases its overheads as a percentage of gross income, thus increasing the net profit. Now, there is a proviso here; making capital expenditures to increase revenue will eat into your net profit, at least temporarily. Your overhead expenses are fixed except for dental supplies and lab expenses. Those last two items are a variable cost. Salary expenses do not generally fluctuate with revenues until you get to the point where you need to add another hygienist or assistant.

Assuming your annual revenue is $800,000, and your practice's operating cash flow is $240,000 (before you deduct your salary and other discretionary expenses), your overhead cost will be $560,000 ($800,000-$240,000) or 70% of your revenues. The question is, how do you decrease that percentage?

If you are not overstaffed, it can often be difficult to trim expenses. For example, if you manage to cut your dental supply costs by 30%, that is, from 10% of revenues to 7%, your overhead is only reduced by 3%. That's not a lot, and I can hear you asking, is it worth the effort? Probably not.

Let's get a little imaginative here, shall we? Here's a way that you can drastically reduce the percentage that your overhead cuts into your bottom-line profit. If you increase your collections from $800,000 to $1 million, your 70% overhead will drop to 60%. By doing so, you will increase your income by 40%, from $240,000 to $400,000. Increasing revenues simply makes more sense. A word of caution; my numbers assume that all expenses remain the same except for the variable cost of dental supplies and laboratory costs, which in this case I assumed to be 20% of collections.

The takeaway here is: don't chase nickels and dimes trying to cut your overhead, focus instead on boosting revenues.

A Good Office Manager is Key to Boosting Practice Profitability

The dream of making an extra half million dollars when you sell your practice probably feels like just that, a dream. When do you have time to even think about maximizing its value? You have a full appointment schedule, patients are waiting weeks to see you even for minor treatments, and you must hustle just to keep up. Lunch breaks have shrunk to a visit to the washroom, a wolfed-down sandwich, and antacids for dessert. Planning for the future is limited to getting out of the clinic before darkness falls.

It doesn't have to be like that. Business savvy dentists are discovering the power and value of employing a well-trained office manager. You can either advertise for an experienced manager or promote from within if you have a senior team member that could potentially fill the role.

First, let's be clear as to what an office manager is and is not. Just because someone is given the title it doesn't mean they are necessarily going to be able to deliver the goods. I have seen many poorly run clinics that have an "office manager" or at least someone referring to themselves by that title. A true office manager must effectively manage the day-to-day operation of the practice. They deal with routine staff issues, perform bookkeeping tasks, and above all ensure that the clinic is humming along smoothly. Within these general areas they should develop or maintain a customized office manual containing job descriptions including job specific expectations, performance-based evaluations, and salary reviews. This will allow the owner/dentist to focus on their job which is looking after the dental needs of patients and, of course, bringing more money into the practice. An office manager should never become a go-fer.

A good office manager is worth every penny you pay them. Hiring a person in this role is only the first step; you need to ensure they receive all the formal training they need. Equipping them with the tools they'll require to improve your bottom line is vital. Think of this as an investment in your future, the practice's future, and not least the amount of money you'll make when you sell the practice.

Training should focus on helping your office manager become a first-class leader who can maintain a happy and motivated team, manage the clinic's bottom line, ensure the practice is delivering exceptional customer service, and attract new patients while reducing attrition.

Most importantly, a top-notch office manager must know how to manage staff, resolve conflict, and effectively deal with all the problems they will encounter daily. They know, and will demonstrate to you, that your staff are not just a salary expense; they are also the key to practice success.

With the goal of improving the bottom line, your office manager's job will include:

- Preparing a business plan that outlines how you will achieve your goal of increasing revenue targets.

- Analyzing monthly income statements to compare projected targets to final figures.

- Setting up efficient clinical and administrative systems across all areas of the operation.

- Managing the practice's overhead.

- Setting daily patient scheduling targets.

- Monitoring patient retention and treatment plan acceptance.

- Implementing an effective social media marketing strategy.

Establish Good Management Systems

Today's buyers will have done their homework or employ advisors that know what to look for in a practice. They will know that you can't have a well-managed clinic without an up-to-date dental practice management system. Before you contemplate selling, you should ensure that all your systems accurately measure the practice's performance. This will allow you to identify areas that require immediate remedial action. Hopefully, your practice already tracks—among other things—office overhead, treatment acceptance rate, dentist and hygiene productivity, your conversion rate when turning inquiries into appointments, and your monthly new patient count. If it doesn't, what are you going to tell prospective buyers?

Check all your systems ahead of selling. Is everything well documented? Does every staff member know what to do, and how to do it? A great way to impress a potential new owner is to pull together a procedures manual that includes front desk processes for billings and collections, hygiene appointments, recall procedures, and just about anything else that needs to be done systematically. Oh, and every employee should have a job description. Why is this important? There is always the chance an employee may leave once a new dentist takes over, however well-planned your transition. Well-documented systems will help get new employees up to speed quickly, so the new dentist can focus on the transition. Don't underestimate these as strong selling points. It's these things, among others, that will help you maximize the value of your practice.

Use Key Monitors to Ensure Practice Success

Management guru Peter Drucker said, "If you cannot measure it, you cannot improve it."

It's hard to imagine driving a car without a speedometer, warning lights, or even GPS. These days we rely on a wide range of safety features that monitor everything the car does: warning lights and buzzers go off if we try to change lanes and there is a vehicle too close, backup cameras ensure we don't hit something, even our steering wheel vibrates if we drift out of our lane. But dentists often run their practices as if they were driving a car wearing a blindfold.

Wouldn't it be good if you had something that shuddered, or set off an alarm when your practice drifted away from high profitability toward losing money or value? The good news is that such a warning system is not only available, but also not a high-end luxury item. With the assistance of your office manager, you can create your own dashboard and instrument panel that will monitor your Key Performance Indicators (KPIs). KPIs analyze various aspects of your clinic to help you make better decisions that in turn improve profitability. They alert you as to whether you are on track or need to take remedial action.

For example, the KPIs for revenues and expenses are:

Overhead	55% of revenues
Salaries	23% of revenues
Clinical supplies	7% of revenues
Lab fees	8% of revenues

Here are a few other KPIs you can measure. Feel free to add as many as you like that are relevant to your practice.

New patients

Target: Convert 95% of phone inquiries into appointments.

Are you tracking incoming inquiries from potential patients, from your website for instance, and calculating your conversion rate? With today's software it isn't difficult to compile this data. If you are, you are in the minority. Industry specialists estimate that dental receptionists can unknowingly turn away as many as one-third of prospective patients. Think about that for a moment. How does it make you feel that despite your strong brand image, reputation, marketing, and social media strategies—all of which encourage people to call your clinic—that one in three prospects are lost because they were not handled correctly?

A failure to convert prospects into patients is the Achilles' heel of most dental clinics and results in huge losses in revenues. The good news is that this issue can be remedied by simply giving your receptionist the right training, and then encouraging them to focus on bonding with each prospective patient on the first call.

Active patients

Target: Reduce your patient attrition rate to less than 10% of your active patient base.

Most dentists keep track of the number of new patients joining their practices, but they seldom count the number of patients who leave. Unfortunately, this might be a case of out of sight, out of mind. Why is this important? Let's assume you have 2,000 active patients and that you are attracting thirty new patients a month, but you are not showing an increase in revenues. This would indicate that your attrition rate is about 1.5% (i.e., about thirty patients), evidenced by the fact that you are not witnessing an increase equivalent to your average per client expected revenue multiplied by thirty. Your target in this case is to cut attrition rates.

There are many ways to encourage active patients to stay with the practice. One of the methods is to make the hours of the practice more convenient. This can depend on your location, however. Many clinics have not only maintained their existing patient base but also increased the flow of new patients by opening on non-traditional hours, including workdays until nine p.m., Saturdays, and perhaps even Sundays.

Maximize treatment acceptance

Target: 90% of patients accept the treatment plan offered.

For many clinics, the ratio of treatment presented, versus treatment accepted, is around 70%. If patients are accepting fewer than seven out ten treatment plans presented to them, you have a problem. The loss of potential revenue this represents will impact your bottom line significantly. There can be many reasons for a low acceptance rate and the first thing to do is a post-mortem with staff each time a patient decides not to proceed. Write down the results of each meeting and look for patterns. It is unlikely that each refusal is different, there will be a commonality. Once you discover what it is, then you can take steps to prevent future occurrences.

Here are the two most common causes:

- Not enough time spent with the patient building trust and explaining the treatment required and how necessary or desirable the course of action is that you are recommending.

- Flexible financing options were not offered, or fully explained.

No-shows

Target: Reduce the no-show rate to 2%.

The no-show rate at the average dental practice is between 4% and 6%, which is not optimal. However, there are several ways you can reduce that percentage. One of the best ways is to email or text patients one or more times leading up to their appointment. Many patients simply forget they have an appointment, especially if it was booked six months earlier.

Making it clear that you charge a fee for no-shows, or last-minute cancellations, can also make people aware of the importance of showing up for appointments. The fee, or course, is somewhat of an empty threat. If you tried to enforce it the patient would probably simply leave the practice. Of course, for a multiple offender, or difficult patient, that might not be such a concern.

Booking appointments

Target: Have 90% of active patients schedule their next appointment before they leave the clinic.

This is often easier for hygiene patients because their next appointment will be several months in the future and their calendars are going to be more open. However, this can also mean they don't see a sense of urgency in making the booking. One way to encourage them is to mention that since they are booking so far in advance, they can have a wide choice of day and time. For many people this can be a huge benefit. For general dentistry, a little patience and encouragement can overcome any hesitancy in booking a specific date. Simply making it a focus of the practice to secure next appointments will have a positive effect on the percentage of patients committing for their next visit.

Waiting times

Target: Ensure patients don't wait longer than ten minutes past their appointment time.

There is a cost of running late. Studies have shown that patients are less likely to refer a friend to your practice for every ten minutes they have been kept waiting. Once again, with hygiene patients this is easier as you usually know exactly how long a patient will take with a specific hygienist. The rest is all about time-management. If your hygienists continually run late then you have a problem that needs to be addressed. It's possible that the amount of time allotted for these appointments is insufficient, which can easily be rectified. If it is a particular hygienist that is always falling behind, then you need to talk to that person and perhaps either help them with time management internally or find some external training. Inefficiency costs money and can devalue a practice.

Inactive patients

It is always less expensive to get past patients back to your practice than it is to acquire new ones. Reactivation is the name of the game. An average clinic may, with a little effort, achieve a 20% reactivation rate, but with the right strategy and a good script you can easily double that percentage.

First, define "inactive patient." Is it someone who you haven't seen in three years? Longer? That's often where practices start when they decide to woo back patients. If they do, their success rate is modest. I suggest starting with those who have not been in the clinic for the last twelve months. The more time away, the less likelihood you have of getting them back. That's not say you shouldn't make the attempt, just not initially. It's the old story of harvesting the low hanging fruit first.

Initial re-contact can be done by phone, email, or snail mail. But voice-to-voice over the phone will always win out. If you haven't got a specific staff member (one with the gift of the gab) responsible for this important activity, you need to think who amongst your staff might be best suited to the job and get them trained. This is a sales role, so the person needs to be persistent but professional, have the ability to generate trust, be a good listener, and most importantly enjoy the job. They need to be upbeat and positive. You will also need to empower them to incentivize your old patient. The incentive could be a free exam or hygiene appointment, or even just the offer of a financing option for the next dental treatment.

Build and maintain a strong team

A dedicated, experienced staff is a key asset in the eyes of a purchaser. Long-term staff members who helped you create your practice's goodwill can transfer that goodwill to a new dentist if they have sufficient incentive. Clearly communicating your vision to your employees will strengthen your team and keep staff sufficiently motivated to support you before and during the practice transition.

To ensure your team is a strong asset in the sale of your practice, you need to "clean house" well in advance of looking for a purchaser. Remove any dead wood several months prior to listing your practice, and build a high-performance, dedicated team that will impress potential buyers.

If, after reading the last two chapters, you feel motivated to reinvent your practice and take it from average—or maybe even good—to being one of the top 10% of practices in the country, bite the bullet and do it all at once, not piecemeal. It's like restoring a vehicle; all the pieces need to be in place to make it run. If you have the luxury of a little time before you plan to sell, you can maximize your selling price by following the advice in this chapter. Do it right and your practice might be worth three times what you thought.

3

Choosing the Right Transition Model

To paraphrase an old song, there are fifty ways to leave your practice. Okay, that's a wild exaggeration, but there are six common transition models you should consider. Here is a brief overview to help you choose the most appropriate for your circumstances.

The Complete Sale

Sell and leave

By far the easiest transition is a straightforward retirement sale. It's ideal if you are planning to retire from dentistry within the next three years. You get the cash, and you hand over the keys to the clinic, just as you would with any real estate deal. In many cases, the closing date of the transaction is the last day you will be working in the practice. It marks the end of your career as a dentist.

Other than being asked for the occasional patient re-treatment, there will be no reason to visit the clinic. This type of walk-away transition is necessary if the patient base can only support one dentist, or if the clinic space is too small for two dentists. You will hope that you have chosen a successor who will care for your patients and staff in the same way you did, but at the end of the day it is no longer your concern.

If the practice is larger, the seller will usually request you stay for a period after the sale, on a part-time basis at least. This will accommodate a smooth transition and gives you an opportunity to ensure your patients receive good continuity of care. Your role will be one of part-time associate and you will be remunerated based on a pre-agreed percentage of your collections.

Sell and keep working

For many dentists, running a practice is the first thing that loses its appeal. They still love dentistry but it's all the other daily hassles that are getting them down. If that describes you, and in an ideal world you'd like to work for another five to ten years, you can sell your practice and work as an associate. In this scenario, you receive the proceeds from the sale and continue earning as an associate until you are ready to hang up your mask and gown.

From the buyer's perspective, how does this arrangement benefit them? On the face of it the buyer paid a great deal of money to get an annual return on his or her investment and there you are taking a chunk of it right from the outset. And if you are doing that, how does the buyer pay the bills and service the debt? They will have to build up the practice as quickly as possible to generate sufficient income to make the loan payments and pay for living expenses. The well-known practice broker Roger Hill refers to this arrangement with Texan humor as "Selling the cow and keeping the milk."

Another disadvantage of this model is that having the seller working as an associate in the clinic can make it more difficult to transition the patients to the new owner.

There are some advantages to the buyer. First, the seller is more likely to finance them, if necessary. Second, there will be no patient attrition because the seller is remaining. Third, knowing that patients are being cared for, allows the buyer more time to focus on marketing.

The Delayed Sale

The delayed sale is a variation of the complete sale. In this scenario you hire an associate to purchase with the agreed-upon goal that they purchase the practice at a pre-determined date. The advantage to you in this arrangement is that you keep control and can sell the clinic at a future date for more money. This option works well if you plan to sell the practice within a three-to-seven-year time frame. Obviously, the clinic must be big enough for two full-time dentists.

The purchase and sale arrangements are made in advance, negating the need for further negotiations down the line. The methodology of establishing the purchase price is also agreed from the outset, and it takes into consideration inflation, lease renewals, projected growth, overhead increases, each dentist's percentage of their production, and anything else that might be pertinent.

Once you have an agreement, the prospective buyer works with you in the practice as an associate. When the sale occurs, the roles are swapped. This type of transition requires three contracts: the associate agreement with the buyer, the purchase and sale agreement, and an associate agreement between the buyer and you after the purchase closes. An overarching agreement should also provide for an initial honeymoon period of three to six months from when the associate starts work. This allows either you or the associate (buyer) to terminate the purchase and sale agreement without penalty.

In exchange for you not listing your practice, you would ask the associate to put down a substantial deposit or a promissory note. If the associate does not purchase your practice, then you would be able to demand payment on the promissory note for the deposit.

In some cases, your practice may not be busy enough to support both of you initially, so the new dentist may choose to supplement their income by working part-time in other clinics.

The advantage of arranging purchase details at the beginning of the relationship is that it provides certainty to both parties. You have financial security along with a firm exit date, and you can plan your future accordingly. One potential drawback is that you are no longer complete master of your own ship. You will need to accommodate the whims of a colleague who may, or may not, share your treatment philosophy, or even your management style. You will need to make it abundantly clear that although you are happy to work closely with the associate/buyer, you remain in complete control until the deal is finalized and you "retire" to work as an associate. At that point the shoe is on the other foot, as the saying goes. The practice management is now the responsibility of the person who was, until the day before, your associate. While this can have its downsides, ending your dental career as an associate has its advantages. The money you earn supplements your retirement income while you are relieved of the burden of managing the practice. And you can stop working whenever you wish. So, freedom does have a price.

Partnership

If you have a successful practice and revenues are growing at a rate which necessitates bringing onboard another dentist, you may want to consider selling a partnership interest in your practice. This could be one-third, a half, whatever works for you and circumstances dictate. If the practice continues to grow, you could sell additional partnership interests. This is a sort of hybrid sale where, effectively, you are realizing some of the equity you have built in your practice while still increasing its overall value.

However, a partnership as a business entity is complex. You will need a specialist team to help you set it all up (i.e., a dental CPA, a transition specialist, and an attorney who specializes in setting up these structures for dentists).

While the partners share the tangible assets, e.g., equipment and the patient charts, each partner receives income based on the clinical revenues produced by the partner. The downside is that partnership agreements are complex, so determining a buyout of a partner later can be costly and time-consuming. Therefore, many dentists choose alternative arrangements such as the solo group transition model discussed below.

Solo Group

In this model, you sell a fractional interest in the practice, usually 50%, to an associate who becomes your partner under a cost-sharing arrangement. In this structure, each dentist owns their own practice. This model is great if you need another dentist to handle a growing patient load. It also gives you a partial payout of the equity you have built in the practice.

This arrangement is a facility-sharing arrangement, where two independent practices operate under the same roof with minimal sharing of staff and expenses. The popularity of this practice model lies in the fact that each dentist retains their independence—they get to eat what they kill, and they don't have to split revenues.

Mid-career dentists who are working at or over capacity, but are not ready to retire, particularly like this model. They get an immediate lump sum in their pocket and enjoy reduced practice time—depending on the number of patients and whether they want to reduce their workdays (fewer days means seeing fewer patients who can be transitioned to the new associate).

This is not a sale that goes through on day one; the closing date will need to be flexible depending on how well the associate helps grow the patient base. Once the sale is complete, the clinic houses two independent practices under the same roof. There is no sharing of production. The two dentists have a buy-out agreement in case of death or disability, but there is no commitment that one dentist will be required to purchase the other dentist's practice at some point in the future.

Merger of Practices

If you have a small practice, which may not be saleable on its own, or your lease is running out, you may want to sell the patient charts to a clinic nearby and work part-time as an associate for them. This will enable you to transition patients to the new practice and eventually to a new dentist.

Alternatively, if you plan to work for another five years and you have enough patients to cover a four-day work week, you may want to consider merging with another practice in a larger space. In this case, ensure that you have a long-term lease for the premises.

Successful practice mergers increase production, reduce overhead, increase practice value, and reduce individual workload. When you decide to retire, the other dentist typically agrees to purchase your interest in the practice. Another option is to bring in an associate one year before you retire, and they purchase your portion of the practice and join the remaining dentist as a cost sharing partner.

As with all mergers, they bring the usual challenges of bridging different practice philosophies. The biggest challenge with this model, however, is blending staff from the two individual clinics into one combined practice. It requires great leadership from both owners to affect a painless transition. To avoid conflict, the parties should agree that any new patient who is not directly referred to a specific practice should be allocated based on the first available dental appointment.

Sale to a Dental Service Organization (DSO)

The $64 million question is: does selling to a DSO put more money in your pocket? Let's take a look.

A DSO certainly offers you a premium for your practice when compared to what you would receive in a regular sale. A downside—or not—is that you may be asked to work for several years as an associate. But let's not stray from the financial rewards aspect and compare two scenarios.

Scenario 1: You sell your practice to a DSO and work as an associate for five years.

Scenario 2: You keep the practice for five years and then sell it.

Here's the simple math.

Estimate your total annual practice income for the next five years. Now add the estimated selling price of your clinic in year five. Make sure you write that figure down—don't waste all your hard work.

Now compare this amount to the amount a DSO might offer you right now with you continuing to work as an associate for five years. Write that down and add to it your estimated earnings as an associate for the five years. If you want to get clever, add the interest you will earn on the assets of the sale over that same five-year period.

You will now have two figures that show you approximately how much money you will have at the end of the five years.

However, and it's a big however—it's not just about numbers. There are a bunch of benefits and disadvantages you will need to consider.

Benefits

1. Selling to a DSO eliminates much of the administrative headaches that come with managing a clinic. In case you need reminding, these include hiring staff, handling payroll issues, monitoring practice performance, marketing, dealing with dental suppliers, and more.

2. You no longer need to worry about selling your practice in the future. The deal has been done, you can carry on working until the end of your agreed term (an agreed date), and then fade into a Caribbean sunset.

3. Being free of ownership will give you more time to do all the things you always wished you had time for. After you have seen your last patient,

you can head off to the golf course. Flexible work schedules become a possibility.

4. There's considerable value in not being burdened with decisions surrounding large capital expenditures.

5. You will very likely have access to a bunch of state-of-the-art technology you could only have dreamed of affording when you were the owner.

Disadvantages

Only two, but they are doozies.

1. You are no longer the boss. For most dentists the loss of autonomy is a hard pill to swallow. It will take some adjustment to adopt the "employee" attitude.

2. There's no going back, and you are committed to your long-term associate contract. And, just in case you thought you saw a loophole, the restrictive covenant will also prevent you from working in a nearby practice.

Working With Other Dentists— A Major Consideration

If you choose any transition model, other than selling your practice outright, you will have to work with other dentists. If you always been a lone wolf this might be a challenge, and the same goes for the dentists with which you will have to work. I know of many horror stories of dysfunctional group practices where dentists share the equipment and/or staff, but never share a kind word or even acknowledge their colleague. They no longer have the interests of the practice at heart and just do their own thing. The practice suffers, patients feel the chill in the air, and office morale ceases to exist except for the despair that permeates the atmosphere.

Don't take this lightly. Ask yourself whether you will be able to hack working with another dentist in close quarters. One way to ameliorate this concern is to be extremely diligent when choosing a dentist with whom to partner. You will need to choose a person with whom you are compatible personally, whose values you share, and who aligns with your practice philosophy. The last thing you want is to be continually at loggerheads.

We've looked at several transition models, but before you decide, unless you are doing the straight complete sale, use my favorite decision-making method courtesy of Ben Franklin.

First, take a sheet of paper and add the heading, "The Pros and Cons of Working with Another Dentist," and create two columns. Now, start populating the columns.

Let me help you get started by making some suggestions.

Pros

Working with another dentist will:

- Reduce my work schedule so I can spend more time on continuing education or developing hobbies.
- Allow me to extend clinic hours to evenings and weekends to attract new patients.
- Reduce practice overhead costs.
- Facilitate better staff utilization.
- Help with the high cost of new equipment.
- Will see my patients when I'm not available.
- Share management responsibilities.
- Increase the value of the practice by increasing revenue and reducing overhead.
- Allow me to earn more money without increasing my hours.

Cons

Bringing onboard a new dentist will:

- Take time, effort, and financial investment.
- Potentially give me more management headaches.
- Be difficult in terms of finding a partner with compatible practice philosophies.
- Mean ceding control over my practice.

- Potentially lead to competition rather than cooperation.

- Be difficult to extricate myself from if things do not work out.

Finding the Perfect Candidate

Finding a suitable candidate is critical to the successful outcome of any practice transition, especially when it involves working side by side with another dentist. It takes more than a gut feeling and a vague notion about compatibility to find a great partner.

Ask your staff to prepare a profile of the ideal candidate. Your employees will likely have a deeper and more objective insight into the attributes a new dentist needs to succeed in your practice. With an established set of criteria, your candidate interviews will become more focused, and evaluations will be simplified. Here are a few selection criteria I have used with clients in the past that you may want to include on your list:

1. Production. Discover how productive the candidate is going to be; that is, how much revenue can you expect them to contribute? You should be looking for a high producer who can get a large percentage of treatment plans accepted by their patients.

2. Compatibility. Are your personalities compatible? You both may want to consider taking a test such as the Myers-Briggs Type Indicator.

3. Philosophy. Evaluate the new dentist's view on patient care, professional development, and marketing.

4. Attitude. Does the candidate exude confidence? Would the associate relate well to your patients? What is the candidate's attitude towards staff? There's an old saying, "Hire for attitude, train for skill." You may be talking to a technically brilliant dentist, but if they are obnoxious to staff and patients then the relationship is doomed from the start.

5. Humility. Does the candidate recognize that as a junior associate, they are in a position to learn from you as the senior dentist? Or do they think they know it all? Do they recognize the value of all staff members and what they contribute to the success of the practice?

6. Technical and management skills. In addition to being a good clinician, is your prospective partner interested in joining the management team to ensure the practice's future financial success?

7. Contacts in the community. Is the candidate willing to permanently move to, and be part of, the community?

8. Work ethic. Is the candidate willing to work hard? Do you detect, "fire in the belly?" If the candidate asks how close you are to the golf course, this is not a good omen.

9. Image. Does the candidate project a professional image and have an appealing appearance and personality?

Make Sure You Have a Thought-out Transition Plan

If you are planning to work with another dentist, give yourself plenty of time and work with advisors to find the most suitable transition model for your personality and situation. Be sure you listen to your accountant regarding the tax implications associated with each choice.

Before you implement your transition plan, make sure you have nailed down the details. For instance, if your would-be successor joins the practice as an associate without having to make a financial commitment, there is a chance they will not follow through with the transition arrangement you have in mind.

Do not delay purchase negotiations until you are close to retirement—it diminishes your negotiating power. An associate who knows you are about to retire will realize that you are in a time crunch and that you will do almost anything to avoid restarting the transition process.

This puts your associate in a power position. You don't want to put yourself in a position of facing The Godfather, Don Vito Corleone, and hearing, "I'm going to make him an offer he can't refuse." Under these circumstances, you will likely end up with a sale price and terms you would have found unacceptable had you negotiated the deal a few years earlier.

4

Planning the Practice Sale

Before you put it on the market, there are several issues you will need to address to get your practice in order. If you decided to sell your house, you would come up with a long list of things you needed to do to get it ready for sale. You'd hire a real estate agent to value it, maybe get a stager to make it look good, and a dozen other things. The same is true when you choose to sell your practice. There are several things you must do before you take the leap. In this chapter, I'll discuss the important ones.

Review Your Facility Lease

The ideal lease arrangement from a purchaser's point of view is a ten-to-fifteen-year term that includes lease renewal options. If your lease has less than ten years to run, get your landlord to agree to additional renewal periods before you put your practice on the market.

Many leases have demolition or relocation clauses; unfortunately, these can be potential deal breakers. Do a little homework and ensure there are no barriers preventing you from assigning your lease to a prospective purchaser. Beware of any personal lease guarantees, these should be removed when the lease is assigned to the new owner.

Review Your Associate Agreement

If you have an associate, make sure that you have an associate agreement in place. This should contain a restrictive covenant, as well as a non-solicitation clause that prevents the associate from taking existing patients and staff members with them should they decide to leave post-sale. Cover your bases so that you don't have to fight a rearguard action during negotiations.

The Practice Valuation

Whether you are selling your clinic privately or through a broker, the first order of business is to have your practice valued. A practice valuation is the key document in the transition process. It provides credibility and backs up your selling price, signaling to buyers that you know the true value of your practice. Banks require this for financing, and it also helps your accountant finalize the tax planning.

Most dentists think that a practice valuation is based on an objective assessment of the practice. It contains a great number of scientific-looking formulas and math; however, when it comes right down to it, the value placed on the practice is subjective—it is the opinion of the valuator. Unlike in the real estate industry, practice sale information is not in the public domain. So where can you get a true idea of the value of your practice? The best source for obtaining accurate, fair market values is from a practice broker. It would be wonderful if they shared the history of practice sales on their websites like real-estate agents, but alas that does not happen. This is why many dentists choose a broker to prepare their valuation. However, when using a broker as both the valuator and the listing agency, the broker can be tempted to over value the practice to "win" the listing. Of course, if the practice sells at the inflated price, you, and the broker both win. However, as is often the case, if it sits on the market for an extended period, you will end up having to accept a price that was lower than you anticipated.

Then there's the question of whether you should go the FSBO route (For Sale By Owner).

FSBO or Broker?

If you have a well-established practice in a great location, you may from time to time receive unsolicited purchase offers. If this is the case, you have the option of dealing directly with the potential buyer and saving a ton of commission. You certainly know your practice better than anyone, and you can get a valuation carried out so that you will have an idea of what your practice should bring in. But, as mentioned above, there is a difference between an objective professional valuation and your practice's true market value. Remember, in order to sell your practice, you will need a professional valuation prepared by a reputable practice broker who is accepted by the lending institution.

Ask yourself two questions, first: will I be happy getting the price a professional valuator puts on the business? The second is, might I, in retrospect, feel I left money on the table by not getting a second "fair market price" valuation?

Going back to our real estate analogy, homes in a hot market often sell at above their assessed value. Dental practices can also sell above what the straightforward valuation suggests. Practice brokers know the current market conditions in your specific market. They will also be able to access a larger group of prospects, and they have the advantage of also being seasoned negotiators, although with that last point you should choose your broker carefully.

If you are still struggling with which choice makes more sense here are several reasons why I suggest using the services of an experienced practice broker.

You avoid stressful negotiations

Clinic owners can agree with their broker on a fair market price and then let the broker negotiate the sale of their practice. By hiring a professional to deal with contentious issues such as price, you avoid uncomfortable situations with fellow dentists, one of whom may become your associate, after you've haggled over purchase price. Basically, brokers make your role as seller a heck of a lot easier and less time-consuming.

You avoid the tire-kickers and fence-sitters

Dealing with prospective buyers is frustrating, as many dentists who went the FSBO route will attest. Many have sent confidential information to a prospect without receiving the courtesy of a response. Or they may find themselves tortured with endless requests for more information, while making no obvious progress on the sale. This is common, especially when there is only a solitary prospective buyer for the practice. The longer the process takes, the greater the chance that the deal will fail. A broker with broader connections will usually have multiple candidates looking at a clinic.

You decrease your chances of failure

The sale of your dental practice is likely one of the most important financial dealings of your career. Since you will probably only ever sell one practice, it's doubtful that you will benefit by learning from your mistakes. A qualified practice transition expert has the expertise to help you win on your first try. When dentists rely solely on attorneys and accountants, who have limited experience in the dental practice sale process, quite often the transition fails.

You get a more compatible candidate

As discussed in previous chapters, transitioning a new dentist to work with your patients and staff will proceed far more smoothly if you and your associate, or partner, share the same traits, practice philosophy, and values. An experienced transition specialist, like any good matchmaker, should be able to find a dentist who meshes well with your practice environment.

You keep your dealings confidential from staff and patients

Most dentists choose not to involve their staff during negotiations, to keep the financial details of the sale confidential. This becomes a challenge if you deal directly with prospective buyers. A transition expert is better placed to maintain confidentiality.

Assembling Your Transition Team

It is critical that your entire transition team is experienced in dental practice sales. If you are not completely confident that your existing advisors, accountants, or attorneys have what it takes to bring together a winning deal, you would be wise to retain a transition expert.

Remember, selling a practice is a once-in-a-lifetime experience; it is no time for amateurs. Just as people form an impression about you from the way you dress, prospective buyers and their advisors will judge you by the professional team handling your sale. Placing a transition heavyweight on your team sends a message to the buyer that there is no room for game-playing, and it communicates that you are a serious seller.

Don't begin the transition process without having your professional team in place. Many dentists only seek advice from experts after the transition process has already gone off the rails. Having them onboard from the outset greatly improves your chances of a successful and profitable outcome.

When selecting a professional team, seek personal recommendations. Make a list of at least three candidates for each spot on your team: an accountant, an attorney, and a dental transition broker—and interview each one. Ask about their experience in practice transitions. Get comfortable with your team of professionals, and never forget that while you should listen to their advice, you have the final say on any major decisions.

The CPA (Certified Public Accountant)

Involve your CPA in the following:

- Preparing practice cash-flow statements for the valuator.

- Preparing cash flow projections for the prospective buyer. This allows them to determine whether the expected cash flow will cover practice expenses, loan repayments, and personal living expenses.

- Tax planning to ensure that you pay the least amount of tax on the sale.

Many dentists believe their accountants are superbly qualified because they have prepared their financial statements for several decades and minimized their tax burden. Yes, they may be saints, but that doesn't make them qualified to lead your transition team. Intimate market knowledge in the world of dental practice sales is essential. Remember, as I discussed earlier, a standard business valuation is not the same as assessing and reaching a fair sales price for your practice in today's market. The latter takes into consideration a multitude of factors including current inventory and availability of similar practices in relation to the number of potential buyers, among other things. Your accountant will have little to no knowledge of the true price your dental practice might attract. Don't let them give an "expert" opinion on practice value.

The attorney or lawyer

Your legal representative should:

- Provide advice on and prepare the letter of intent.

- Review legal agreements (these are usually prepared by the buyer's solicitor) to ensure that the requested representations are not too onerous, and your financial obligations are minimized after the closing date.

- Review your current lease agreement for the premises and make arrangements to reassign the lease to the buyer.

The dental transition broker

The transition broker is the quarterback on your team. You should expect your broker to get you the best price for your practice and advise you on how to professionally approach the sale. A good broker should be practical, no-nonsense, creative, and adept at keeping costs down. They should also understand that any proposed transition deal will only succeed if financial and tax benefits are maximized for the seller and buyer alike.

Your dental transition broker will:

- Prepare a transition plan that meets your long-term financial objectives.

- Prepare a practice valuation and a marketing prospectus.

- Find the most suitable candidate or associate.

- Screen potential buyers.

- Assist in all sale negotiations.

- Assist your legal counsel as required.

- Structure co-ownership arrangements.

Shall I Sell the Real Estate with the Practice?

Almost every prospective practice buyer would like to own the real estate as well. It is a good investment because the buyer becomes both landlord and tenant. And even more so because many dentists have had bad experiences fighting with landlords over leases. There are many points of potential friction with a landlord. Not getting a renewal of the lease, or issues with assignment of the lease to another dentist are just a couple. The landlord is also able to destroy the goodwill of your practice by invoking the demolition clause, or by forcing you to relocate to another part of the building.

Taking this into consideration, it will come as no surprise that a buyer will pay a premium for your practice if they are also able to own the real estate. If you own the property but don't want to sell it to your practice buyer, and insist instead on leasing the space to them, you may find your buyer cool to the idea. Generally, buyers are not keen on becoming tenants of the seller.

Why? If the seller was to cancel the lease for any reason, or they simply don't renew it, then they can take over the assets (e.g., leasehold improvements, fixtures and fittings, and goodwill attached to the clinic location) of the dental clinic without paying a dime.

Often the selling dentist is willing to sell the real estate with the practice. In many cases, however, the buyer does not have the borrowing power with their bank to finance both the clinic and the real estate. As a result, a seller may grant an option to the buyer to purchase the real estate at some point in the future when the bank is willing to finance the purchase.

Give Your Clinic a Facelift

We live in a consumer-oriented world. Today's patient is more knowledgeable, more demanding of good customer service, and increasingly aware of their value and the power they hold. Their expectations regarding a dentist's skill, overall attentiveness of staff, the functionality and efficiency of the practice, and of course their own comfort, has never been higher.

At the same time, competition has never been greater for the patronage of patients. Long gone are the days when you could design the practice for you and your staff, and virtually ignore the patient. Excessive wait times, when demand exceeded supply, and patients being lucky to be able to get in to see a dentist are things of the past. Take a long, hard look at your clinic. Does it look sterile, dated, cramped? A young, keen, new dentist will immediately look at a dated practice and start calculating how much it will cost to update. Then they will add all the time and inconvenience it will also cost them. One of two things will then happen. They will either walk to the next practice for sale on their list or offer you a lowball price. Take it from me, it will most likely be the former.

Think about it from the patient's perspective. Why should they choose you over one of the other clinics in town? There is a lot of choice. Increasingly, forward-thinking clinics are reinventing themselves. They are transforming what has often been a dull, sterile atmosphere lit with harsh fluorescents, into one that features natural, yet luxurious decor. Materials such as hardwoods, stone, and plants are highlighted, and using accent lighting creates a calming ambiance. It is these clinics that inspire confidence in patients and potential buyers alike. There are dental practices that feature coffee shops, jukeboxes, eco-friendly green walls, the latest touchscreen televisions, and massive aquariums. There are themed clinics catering to children such as Aurora

Borealis Orthodontics in Toronto. It not only features Star Trek movie props, but patients can lie back and look at the stars above. And, of course, it features "out of this world smiles"—how cool is that?

Will Rogers said, "You never get a second chance to make a first impression." Your new patient's first impression is based on your office and the greeting they receive from your staff, long before they get an opportunity to judge your skills and professional conduct as a dentist. Why would your prospective buyer be any different? The moment they step through your door they are either going to think that this might be good value, or poor value. A bargain, or a practice they might get for a bargain price. Or, one they can't wait to walk away from.

Today's buyers realize the power of design as a key building block for practice success, and they know that:

- Patients demand a more comfortable and soothing environment.

- It will increase patient referrals.

- It sets a practice apart from the "vanilla" clinics in the neighborhood.

- It tells the public how the practice values its patients.

- It reduces stress and makes the workplace a healthier environment.

- It increases productivity, helping the office run more efficiently.

Surveys have shown that many patients, and potential new owners, now realize that patients see the clinic design and decor as a reflection of the competence of the dentist and the practice as a whole. This has resulted in an upswing of dentists renovating their practices to make them more attractive and comfortable for patients. I recommend that you carry out a little research and see what state-of-the-art dentists are doing to attract patients and bring dentistry into the 21st century.

If your clinic has a worn-out look but you don't feel it needs—or you can't stomach—a total renovation, consider enhancing the "curb appeal" of your practice. It doesn't need to cost a fortune to upgrade office technology, recover chairs, replace carpets, and spiff up the facility with some fresh paint and landscaping.

Remember, this is an investment, it is not wasting money to benefit the new owner. Modern, hip practices sell for more. Period.

When Do You Tell Your Employees?

The short answer is, very early on in the process. There are very few upsides to playing things close to your chest, and a ton of downsides. In my experience, some dentists start thinking out loud about retiring long before they are seriously contemplating selling. This becomes a self-inflicted, pernicious rumor. Your employees will start talking amongst themselves about whether you are trying to sell the practice. They will worry about their job security. They may start looking for another job to be on the safe side. Heaven forbid they might even start mentioning their fears to patients. All because you mused. Don't muse! The last thing you want is for your practice transition to crash and burn, with staff and patients abandoning ship before you have even decided that you want to sell.

On the other hand, keeping silent while working on a deal is even worse—if that is possible. Imagine the following scenarios—and if you think these are flights of imagination, think again, these actually happened; you secretly sell and parachute the new dentist into the clinic (to everyone's surprise) one Monday morning. Listen to this imaginary exchange between a patient and one of your assistants.

Patient: *I didn't know you had a new dentist. He's not the new owner, is he?*

Assistant: *Neither did I, until about an hour ago. Yes, we were quite shocked when we heard the news that he was taking over. To be honest, I'm not sure what I am going to do. I'm considering looking for a job elsewhere.*

Sounds bad, doesn't it? I remember a practice sale that crashed and burned spectacularly the day the new owner took over. Both the outgoing and incoming dentists could have starred in a *How Not to Sell Your Practice* video on YouTube. If it hadn't been so serious for the innocent people affected, it would have been funny. Let's hear it from the perspective of Sally, who had been my client's assistant for ten years.

"It was a Monday morning, much like any other—at least at first. Bob gathered us around and introduced us to the new owner. I was stunned, I just stood there speechless and looked around at my colleagues. A bunch of ash white faces looked back. If looks could kill, Bob would have keeled over right then and there. I took an instant dislike to the new guy; he didn't make eye contact and looked nervous. No doubt the unsmiling faces that confronted him didn't help. I hated how happy Bob looked—it was almost like he was gloating, rubbing his hands together imagining all the money he'd made, while throwing all of us under the bus. Maybe, if the new guy had tried to be friendly, we would have all felt a little more positive, but the first thing he did was ask Patty, our receptionist, to train his wife to take over her job. Way to go, he's been here for five minutes, and Patty is told to train her own replacement? After the awful meet and greet, we managed to grab a moment here and there to talk amongst ourselves. We all resigned just after lunch. The new boss was only our boss for a few hours. And Bob, we renamed him Judas. He obviously cared more about money than the long-standing relationship we had with him—obviously that was all a sham."

The bitterness in Sally's words is obvious, as is the contempt she feels for her former boss, and colleague, Bob. As the clinic was housed in a professional building, there were several other practices hiring. As known entities, Bob's employees were popular. The new owner had to use his checkbook to buy the loyalty of a few staff members and get them to stay until he could find replacements. I'd like to say it all worked out in the end, but the practice never recovered and a year later the new owner sold it at a loss.

Imagine what might have happened if Bob had worked with his team from the outset and involved them in helping him choose a suitable successor. A person the staff liked, respected, and who they felt would be well received by patients. How would that conversation between patient and dental assistant have gone?

Patient: *I didn't know you had a new dentist. She's not the new owner, is she?*

Assistant: *Yes, she is. It took us almost a year to find the right person with the same philosophy as Dr. Green and who we were sure would have a great attitude towards our patients. You are really going to like her.*

If Bob had involved his staff, they would have made the transition easy and ensured that patients were more positive about the changes and that the attrition rate was minimal. A lot of the goodwill in any practice comes from the staff. Here's a thought, maybe you should consider offering them a percentage of what that goodwill earned you in the sale? After all, they earned it.

The common belief in the dental industry is to keep the sale a secret from patients and the employees. Dentists are led to believe that by informing staff and patients beforehand they will jeopardize the sale of the practice, as it would create uncertainty for staff and patients, and potentially trigger an exodus to another clinic.

The reality is that over the years you created a deep, trusting relationship. Employees would feel honored if you asked them to work together to ensure a smooth transition. Your staff will also tell you whether the new dentist is a good fit and would be accepted by the patients. The buyer knows that the existing staff is critical for the future success of the clinic. When you are in your sixties, your patients anticipate that you would be selling your clinic someday soon. They have no reason to leave the practice. It will be up to the new dentist to create the same trust relationship with them as you did. Your patients will also appreciate that you give them the opportunity to complete the proposed treatment plan.

5

Dealing with the Prospective Buyer

The Marketing Prospectus

Initially, prospective buyers have limited information to go on, usually just enough to whet their appetite. For instance: approximate location, revenues, number of operatories, and price. The purpose of the one-page prospectus is to summarize the opportunity by providing enough additional information (without disclosing your identity) to ensure that only serious buyers will decide to move on to the next stage. It's a bit of a balancing act. You don't want everyone and their dog knowing that you are selling—such as competitors, suppliers, staff, etc.—but you do want to attract the right potential buyers. The two main parts of the prospectus are the practice profile and a financial summary.

Practice profile

Without getting into too many details, provide an overview of the relevant features of your practice, including square footage, description of the facility, history of gross revenues and net income, lease terms, number of active patients who have attended the practice over the last twelve to eighteen months, monthly average of new patients, and a staff profile showing hours worked per week and salaries.

Keep in mind that the prospectus is a selling tool. Emphasize the features which distinguish your practice from others in the community. List your competitive advantages such as low overhead, implementation of new technology, first-class location, and above average new patient count.

Financial summary

The financial summary pitches why the deal makes sense financially. It answers the buyer's most burning question, "What will my actual take-home income be?" Provide projections of the practice's net income and cash-flow that clearly show it generates sufficient funds, comfortably covering living expenses and servicing the debt on a purchase loan. The goal of the financial sales pitch is to make the buyer feel comfortable and secure in the knowledge that your practice will meet their financial needs.

Practice Visit

After reviewing your prospectus and studying the practice valuation, prospective buyers who are interested will ask to see your practice. It is important that you attend the showing with your broker. Your presence as the owner-dentist at this phase of the transition is invaluable. The most successful transitions occur when buyer and seller hit it off instantly.

Discover as much as you can about the prospect prior to the office tour. It's amazing how much a simple Google search can uncover. Commenting on the buyer's career and hobbies, awards, volunteer work etc., are all great icebreakers. It almost instantly creates a trust relationship. Discussions with the buyer provide an opportunity to shape the offer the buyer will make. For example, you could talk about the amount of time you plan to spend with the associate after the sale to orient them to the practice. The more comfortable they feel the more likely they are to open their checkbook. During these early discussions, ask the buyer how they see the future. Put yourself in their shoes, what would be important to you? Are they, perhaps, looking to be mentored by you? Do they need a job for their spouse? Is financing to purchase real estate a stumbling block? Do they need help with that or anything else? Understanding a buyer's needs will help you handle unspoken objections. This is a very powerful sales tool and is the grease for a smooth sale.

During the practice visit you will start to see whether you share the same values and philosophy as the buyer. If you do, it will go a long way toward reaching a successful sale and transition. It also helps remove any obstacles which may arise.

Connecting and building a relationship with the buyer can have significant advantages. If, for example, the attorneys start to quibble over sale terms and it looks as though the deal might crash and burn, you may be able to resolve the impasse by speaking directly with the buyer. I have seen many faint-hope situations resolved when a simpatico buyer and seller communicated directly. Unfortunately, this is not always the case, in many practice transitions the seller meets the buyer for the first time on the day the new owner takes over.

Here are thirty-seven questions a buyer might ask you during a practice visit. A little advance preparation pre-visit will reap dividends when you have all the answers at hand.

- What are your reasons for selling, and what is your exit strategy?

- Would you be prepared to work as a part-time associate after the sale?

- Does the practice have an associate? How experienced are they and does the contract have a restrictive covenant?

- What is the current monthly production?

- How many "active" patients do you have? How many patients were seen in the last 18 months?

- Is the practice growing? How many new patients do you see per month?

- What is the average age of your patient base?

- What is the ethnic composition of your patient base?

- How close do the patients live to the dental clinic? What is the likelihood of patients not living close by changing to a different practice after the sale?

- How many patients have left the practice in the last two years, and what were their reasons?

- How prepared is the clinic to handle current patient volume?

- How well does the capacity of the clinic handle the current patient volume?

- How many new patients do you attract through your website?

- Do you have a marketing program? Does it include social media?

- What are the basic lease features, including terms and renewal options? Is there a demolition clause?

- If you own the real estate, is there an option to purchase the building?

- How many operatories are in use? Are any in need of repair?

- Could operatories be added without major renovations?
- Is there adequate parking for staff and patients?
- Is the practice understaffed or overstaffed?
- Are there written office policies regarding vacation, sick time, overtime, salary increases, and benefits?
- Is on-the-job performance evaluated? How often?
- Are salaries comparable to the industry average?
- Are salary increases based on productivity, and if so, how is it measured?
- When was the last salary increase? When is the staff expecting the next increase?
- What employee changes will be required? What is the likelihood some staff members will not stay after the purchase?
- What renovations might be required to improve efficiency?
- Could the practice be relocated at a reasonable cost?
- Is the equipment in good working order?
- What front desk software do you use? Is it up to date?
- What is the collections performance?
- Is the practice charging more than the fee guide?
- What component of the total office production comes from hygienists?
- Is the hygiene component of the practice fully utilized?
- How many hygiene days are there per week?
- What proportion of endodontics, periodontics, oral surgery, and implant placement is referred out?
- How many days do you take off each year?

The day after the practice visit, the broker will send a thank-you note and set up the next step, a telephone call, or follow-up meeting.

It is important to attract as many interested parties as possible. If you deal with just one prospective buyer and they know that nobody else is interested, they will get the impression that the practice cannot be that attractive, because nobody else is eager to buy. At that point, the prospect may lose interest and you might lose the sale, or they may start driving the price down thinking you might be desperate. Competition alters all that; your practice becomes increasingly attractive, and a sense of urgency is generated.

Plan for the Buyer's "Due Diligence"

When you last purchased a house, you probably hired someone to carry out a professional property inspection. Forewarned is forearmed, as the saying goes. If there are issues, knowing about them ahead of time allows you to use them as bargaining chips. Most buyers will carry out a due diligence investigation on your practice. Don't be caught off guard, a buyer may decide to do this at any time. Be ready. It will be carried out by several different people and include a patient chart audit, inspection of the premises and the equipment, and the clinic accounting records.

Your promising sale may be in danger if, for instance, a buyer's equipment specialist reports that repairs are required on several pieces of vital equipment. At that point you and the buyer will have to agree on whether you make the repairs, or they reduce their offer. Any disagreement will see your transition heading for the rocks.

I recall a $1 million practice sale falling apart because of an accounts receivable issue. The problem arose due to patient credit balances. These occur when a patient or insurance company has paid out more than the amount outstanding. A credit balance is essentially a debt to the patient. These amounts are typically quite small, so practices often don't bother with the adjustment unless the patient asks for a reimbursement. While the individual patient balances may be small, the totals can add up if not regularly adjusted. The practice in this story had let the credit balances amount to about $35,000. The buyer insisted he withhold $35,000 from the proceeds, arguing that this was the clinic's debt. The seller argued that the credit balances were old and the practice would likely never have to pay them out. After spending a great deal of money on legal fees, the buyer withheld the $35,000, but agreed to pay the seller back over five years in equal annual installments minus any payments made to patients.

Adopt the Right Frame of Mind

Occasionally, selling a practice can bring the worst out in people. I have witnessed an easy-going, friendly, generous dentist turn into a miser haggling over nickels and dimes. Arguments over the value of a practice's dental supply inventory, or who pays the cost of mailing a letter to patients announcing the new owner, are often petty and always poisonous. Remember your reputation and take into consideration the well-being of your staff and your patients. Follow the advice of the motivational speaker Zig Ziglar: "You can get everything in life you want, if you will just help enough other people get what they want!"

Greed can kill your sale in an instant. Okay, I understand that you put your heart and soul into your practice for many years, it was your baby. It's understandable that you might have a hard time accepting anything less than what you feel it's worth. But if you really want to sell you will need to check your emotions at the door and set some realistic expectations. Now for the hard part—put yourself in the buyer's shoes. Leave some juice on the table for them, it will pay you back in other ways.

6

The Letter of Intent (LOI)

The LOI should not be confused with LOL, although sometimes when you get an LOI you may well LOL. Receiving an LOI is the moment you know that the people who have been sniffing around your clinic, maybe even touring it, are serious. Once you have it in your hands, signed by the interested party, negotiations can begin in earnest. What is the letter of intent exactly? It lays out the basic terms of the deal and is the foundation on which the purchase agreement is built.

A purchase offer for a dental practice is structured in much the same way as that of a residential home. It will include the price, a list of excluded items, and a list of purchase conditions such as inspection and financing. One important thing to remember, is that although it looks official and is a key document in any sale, it is just the buyer's opening salvo. It is a starting point for negotiations and nothing else. Unless, of course, it has a few more zeros than you, or your transition broker expected, but how likely is that?

If your practice has been on the market for a while, you can expect the opening offer to be low—but hopefully not an insult. Even if it is, keep cool. Leave it to your broker or transition specialist to go back to the buyer's representative and give them a dose of reality.

Just like in a house sale, there are certain protocols to follow when you respond to an LOI. The first thing to note is the date by which you must respond. This is important. Very likely the buyer will not give you a lot of time. Their strategy will be to put you under pressure and make it difficult for you to shop the offer around in search of a higher bid. If you are working with a transition specialist, they will help you avoid this situation by being proactive and coordinating offers, giving you the opportunity to review multiple offers and choose the one that represents the best deal for you given your situation.

This coordination of offers has the advantage of alerting potential buyers to the fact that they are not alone—there is competition. And that is healthy—at least for you. In these circumstances, offers close to the going market rate will be presented. If, however, your practice has been on the market for some time and is stale, then a prospect is very likely to be suspicious that it is overpriced. In this case they may walk away or give you a lowball offer.

The Anatomy of the Letter of Intent

A letter of intent is not binding on the buyer except regarding confidentiality and exclusivity. The buyer is obligated to keep all information obtained about your practice, during negotiations, strictly confidential. The only exclusions to this are their professional advisors and other parties such as a bank, and even then, only as necessary to pursue the completion of the purchase. In terms of exclusivity, you agree not to negotiate with other parties with respect to the sale of the clinic until the conditions of the offer are satisfied (by the agreed date). Only if and when the conditions are not satisfied, or the offer is rescinded, or the LOI expires, are you free to negotiate with other buyers. The component parts of an LOI are discussed below.

Purchase price

The LOI stipulates the purchase price and whether it is an asset or stock deal. The former is where the buyer purchases the assets and liabilities (the sum of all assets less the sum of agreed liabilities) of the business; a stock deal is where the buyer purchases the seller's stock in the corporation which owns the practice assets. You will need to talk to your accountant before you decide which route is more beneficial to your circumstances. Much will depend on what makes sense for both you and the buyer. If you disagree, that will become a major factor in the negotiation of the sale.

Another factor concerning price which you should take into consideration, is that not every deal is paid in cash on closing. It is not uncommon to be asked to finance a portion of the purchase price by taking back a promissory note. Should you consider this? If a buyer asks you to finance a substantial portion of the purchase price, I suggest you walk away from the deal.

However, if the buyer needs $200,000 of financing on a million-dollar purchase price, it may be worth considering your options. Promissory notes are a concern. It's always a gamble whether the buyer will be forced to defer repayments, or worse, default on the debt entirely. This is where a little creativity can save a deal. I had a client a few years ago that had a keen buyer for his $1 million practice. In fact, she was the only person interested in purchasing the practice. Unfortunately, the prospective buyer's bank would only agree to loan her $800,000. My client was motivated to sell but not keen to lend the dentist the $200,000 difference. He then came up with the idea of offering to co-sign 20% of the bank loan, to which the bank agreed. To further limit his exposure, after a display of formidable negotiating, he got the bank to agree to apply the loan principal portion of the repayments to the amount he had guaranteed first.

Another purchase price wrinkle is that a buyer may request that a portion of the purchase price is in the form of an "earnout." This strategy involves you continuing to work as an associate during the earnout period. In effect, the buyer withholds a portion of the sale price. This amount is subsequently paid out to the seller over time based on them meeting certain conditions, such as maintaining revenues at a stipulated level. This type of deal only makes sense if the buyer's offer is superior to all other offers because you need to be confident that you will be able to meet revenue targets as laid out in the earnout agreement.

The deposit

Taking an "Earnest Money" deposit of $5,000 or $10,000 shows good faith on the part of the buyer, but in the big scheme of things it is not much money in return for signing the exclusivity clause we discussed earlier. It is a common, and wise, practice to have the deposit increased by perhaps $30,000 or $50,000 when conditions are removed and the letter of intent becomes binding. A word of warning: if the buyer can't come up with the cash, you might want to consider getting a promissory note. Should the deal fall through, you will then at least be in a position to force the buyer to honor the promissory note.

The list of assets

The sale of a practice typically includes the following assets:

- Leasehold improvements and fixtures.

- Office furniture, equipment, computers, hand instruments, hand pieces, etc.

- Inventory and supplies at approximately the same levels as maintained in the ordinary course of business.
- The goodwill of the dental practice, including all patient lists and patient records, financial records, and the right to any trade names, email addresses and websites.

The excluded assets

Certain assets will be excluded, including:

- Accounts receivable.
- Any personal mementos including textbooks and artwork.
- The seller's liabilities, including accounts payable and lease obligations, unless specifically assumed by the buyer.

Accounts receivable

There are two ways to deal with the accounts receivable. Option one is for the buyer to collect the accounts receivable on behalf of the seller for a specified time after the sale and remit the receipts to the seller less a management fee (usually 5%).

Option two sees the buyer purchase the accounts receivable. To reduce the exposure posed by uncollected receivables, the purchase price is often adjusted for potential bad debts. The benefit to the buyer of option two is that it provides immediate working capital. For you, the seller, either course of action is acceptable.

The closing date

In most cases once the LOI is signed the closing date for the sale is set between sixty and ninety days. Sometimes, buyers will request a later closing date because of work commitments. Be warned, the longer the gap between receiving the initial deposit and the closing date, the greater the chance of the deal collapsing. One way to minimize this risk is to increase the deposit so the buyer has more skin in the game.

Non-competition/non-solicitation clauses

These clauses prevent you from practising dentistry within a certain geographic radius of the clinic for a set period. Unless, of course, you are working in the clinic as an associate as part of the sale agreement. They also prevent you from soliciting any employees or patients of the practice after the closing date, should you cease to be an associate of the practice. Basically, you need to be aware that unless you continue working in the clinic, or move beyond the defined geographic region, you will not be able to practice dentistry.

Conditions precedent

Here is a sample of typical conditions that are to the buyer's benefit.

- Approval of the financial statements and other financial information.
- Financing approval.
- Patient charts audit.
- A lease assignment with the buyer. If you own the real estate, you may either offer a long-term lease or offer it for sale. The purchase price is usually based on the appraised value. Alternatively, you can grant an option to the buyer to buy the real estate at some point in the future, or you can give a right of first refusal.
- Satisfactory equipment inspection.
- Satisfactory review of employment agreements.
- Acceptance of seller's associate agreement.

Re-treatments

This provision holds the seller financially responsible for re-treatments, usually up to twelve months after the closing date. The seller has the option to re-treat the patient at the clinic, at no cost.

Goodwill obligations

This provision obligates the seller to assist in an effective transfer of the dental practice's goodwill. It includes distributing a letter introducing the new dentist to patients and referral sources.

Negotiating the Terms of the Letter of Intent

I always think that negotiating the terms contained in an LOI is the most interesting part of the transition process. However, many dentists find it stressful, especially when they receive their first lowball offer after what they felt was a cordial practice visit with a prospective buyer. Or, as can be the case, the buyer rejects their terms for a post-sale associate agreement. The thing is, it's all a game, and in the early days the game involves a whole lot of posturing. So take a deep breath, restrain the urge to tear up the LOI and consign it to the trash bin, and work to negotiate a better deal. Someone once said that the first offer you receive is usually the best. I don't know how true that is but I do know that the next offer might not be a whole lot better and a buyer-in-hand is your best shot of getting a sale—and hey, they expect you to counter.

Think of the LOI as a first step, not a *fait accompli*. In my experience, most dentists don't see themselves as skilled negotiators and are often uncomfortable with the sales process. Unfortunately, the reality is that being a skilled negotiator is vital if you are going to get the concessions and the sale price you want. If you lack the skills, the desire, or the time to devote to negotiating a good deal, you may have more success using a broker or transition specialist. This is not to say that you should not be involved in the sale; remember, a buyer will not invest in your practice unless he or she has established a relationship of mutual trust with you. People only buy from those they trust.

There is an old sales story that talks of the owner of a hardware store instructing a new sales assistant. The owner says to the young woman, "When someone comes in to purchase a drill bit, remember, it's not the drill bit they actually want, it's the hole it makes." In the case of a prospective buyer, they want the income stream which you generate; and that comes from the long-term relationship you have with your patients. The goodwill and hard assets are just the drill bit. Your dental practice is unique to you; for the buyer to step into your shoes, he or she needs to find out as much as possible about you.

Negotiation Tips

Don't get involved in direct negotiations

Every sales trainer will tell you that to be successful in sales you always need to understand what the buyer needs and wants. What is their motivation? What excites them? How can you meet their needs at a price they can afford? The only way to discover all of this is to get to know them by cultivating a relationship during the practice visit and any subsequent meetings. Discover what questions, concerns, and objections they might have about the purchase. Remember, if there is an outstanding objection, one that has been left unresolved, you will never get the sale. Welcome hearing their concerns, and by answering them, build mutual trust. Be as honest and as helpful as possible. However, no matter how well you bond, don't get involved in direct negotiations concerning the sale. I strongly advise you engage an experienced transition specialist to act as a buffer between you and the buyer. Let them handle the difficult conversations free from emotion, negotiate on your behalf, and keep the relationship between you and the buyer intact.

Conduct the negotiations in a cooperative and caring manner

Selling a dental practice is very different to selling a house. When you sell a house, you walk away and don't look back; you may in fact never even meet the buyers in person. When selling your practice, however, maintaining a trust relationship is vital especially if you are going to continue as an associate. Always show humility and respect. Foster a cooperative atmosphere through optimism and enthusiasm. Learn as much as you can about the prospect by listening more and talking less. Greek philosopher Epictetus is attributed as saying, "We have two ears and one mouth so that we can listen twice as much as we speak." Wise words. I suggest you avoid volunteering too much information but answer any questions in a confident, straightforward, and honest way. Then, keep quiet.

Negotiate everything

I have found, when handling transitions, that if both the seller and the buyer bargain hard and the outcome of a tough negotiation results in a mutually satisfactory agreement on all important issues, then both parties are more likely to feel good about the result.

Think about it for a moment, if you listed your dental clinic for $800,000 and the following day a buyer offers the full asking price on the spot, will you feel satisfied? Unlikely. You will naturally think, "Heck, I really left money on the table. I should have asked for more." On the other hand, if after a long-drawn-out negotiation, you settle on $800,000 you will feel victorious. There is something satisfying about reaching a mutually beneficial agreement.

Bring skeletons out of the closet early

If, when you decide to put your practice on the market, you are involved in any legal disputes or you are aware that your premises or equipment need repair, disclose that information immediately. Never let the buyer discover it during the practice visit, or worse, sometime later. The best course of action is to take remedial action immediately. If you fail to be upfront at all times with the buyer, you could jeopardize the sale.

Increase the perceived value of your practice

If the price you are asking is supported by a valuation report and it reflects true market value, but you are still experiencing kickback on the price, then you are probably experiencing a value-proposition perception issue. Basically, the buyer does not feel that what they are buying is worth what you are asking. This can turn into a 6,000-pound elephant in the room, one that is sitting between you and the buyer. It can pose a seemingly insurmountable hurdle.

To overcome this, the best course of action is to add value to the proposition rather than cut price. The more you get to know what motivates the buyer and discover their needs, the better you will be able to add value to the deal. In my experience, the most common areas to do this relate to financing and real estate. Often, buyers are keen to own the practice's real estate, but are unable to get full financing. In this case you might consider offering a seller's mortgage for the shortfall. At other times, it's related to the buyer's circumstances. For instance, if you can solve a major problem they are experiencing, you can make the deal more attractive. I've seen sellers help the spouse of a buyer find work in the community or offer to mentor a young dentist who is concerned about the financial exposure of the purchase due to their inexperience. Solving key issues that are making the buyer nervous adds value to the deal and can overcome price resistance or commitment-hesitancy.

Rather than browbeating the buyer into accepting a deal on your terms, take the time to understand what they want from the deal and devise your negotiation strategy accordingly. As you negotiate the sale, if you experience price resistance, summarize all the benefits of the deal. This will help build value in the buyer's mind. If you know your price is fair, the only deal-breaker is that the buyer fails to "see" the value. In short, never defend price, promote value.

Walk away

Always know your drop-dead price and stick to it. If negotiations become deadlocked and you are being asked to drop below the price you are comfortable with, walk away. Be generous; say that you understand the buyer's position but at the same time make it clear that if the prospect is unwilling to compromise, you are not prepared to sell the practice. Walk away, but always leave the door open. If you don't hear back from the prospect after three business days, you can call back to see if they have changed their mind. The "walk away" strategy is an excellent test to see whether the prospect is willing to increase their purchase offer.

The Purchase and Sale Agreement (Complete Sale)

As I said in the previous chapter, the letter of intent lays out the basic terms of the proposed deal; now things get serious. Since receiving an LOI you will have gone through several rounds of negotiations involving your transition broker, your lawyer, and your CPA. Hopefully, if you've got to the stage of having a purchase and sale agreement drafted, most of the major issues have been ironed out. I say hopefully, because there is a whole lot that can change between the time you verbally agree to everything, and when it becomes locked into the legal agreement. This chapter will help you identify and deal with all the tricky things that can creep into an agreement either innocently, or through the devious machinations of the buyer's advisory team.

Remember, lawyers live in an adversarial environment—they know how to play the game. The last thing you should do is become too emotionally involved, especially with minutiae. If you do, you might end up kiboshing the whole deal. I heard of a case where a seller stubbornly refused to make any concessions, even when advised to do so by their lawyer. In this case it was $1 million sale, and the argument was over who would pay a $10,000 clinic repair bill. In my opinion, it makes no sense to watch a million-dollar payday go south because of an amount that equates to 1% of the value of the deal. Even more so when you consider the additional costs incurred in finding another buyer. Never lose sight of the fact that it's the buyer who will have to spend the next ten years repaying the loan they took out to purchase your practice.

So, what is your role? I realize that for Type A personalities this might be difficult, but your role first and foremost is to be the cheerleader, not to start making last-minute plays. The value of this approach is that it enables you to maintain a friendly and collegial relationship with the buyer. It allows you to say, "Let the lawyers sort out all the nitty-gritty stuff, we know we're agreed on the big picture going forward."

Part of your "cheerleader" role is to help the new dentist take over the care of your patients and employees, and to build on your legacy. All of this is especially important if you are going to stay on as an associate post-sale.

The purchase and sales agreement is shaped to a large extent by the negotiating expertise of the two opposing lawyers. The opposing lawyer naturally has the buyer's best interests in mind, and yours will be trying to ensure you get the best possible deal while minimizing your obligations after the sale. Because the lawyers represent opposing interests, a win-win transition is virtually impossible. What one side loses, the other side gains.

Imagine selling your practice as if it were a steeplechase, the purchase and sale agreement is the final hurdle before you get your large check at the finish line. But hold on there, Red Rum, that final hurdle can be a lot higher and trickier than it looks.

For many dentists, once they receive the purchase and sale agreement, they put their trust in the rest of their team; after all, who has time to read dozens of pages of contract legalese that you've already agreed to? You—that's who! Read it and read it well. If you take only one thing from this book it should be that you skip this step at your own peril.

Sit down in your office or in your study at home, close the door, put up a do not disturb sign, and carefully go through every guarantee you are making and every obligation for which you are agreeing to take responsibility. Before you begin, however, make a list of questions that you would like to see addressed. Here are a few you might want to add to get you started.

1. Is the list of assets that will be included and excluded from the sale correct?

2. If I am selling my clinic's assets, does the price allocated for goodwill, equipment, leaseholds, and other tangible assets help minimize my tax liability? Do I fully understand the explanation given to me by my CPA?

3. Has my exposure to a possibly large expense for re-treating patients been minimized, or eradicated?

4. Am I satisfied with how the accounts receivable will be handled?

5. Does the restrictive covenant relating to patients and employees, that I will be obliged to adhere to, seem reasonable both now and in the future?

6. Are the personal representations and obligations to which I am agreeing reasonable? Do I have any misgivings?

Now, using a copy of the agreement, get yourself a bright yellow highlighter, a pen with green ink, another with red, and read the document thoroughly. First, highlight everything you don't understand so that once you have finished reviewing the document, you can arrange to discuss each of those points with the relevant member of your transition team. With your green pen, put a check mark against, or circle, everything you agree with, and a red cross against anything you didn't agree to during negotiations. And finally, highlight anything that isn't 100% clear.

I have come across dentists who failed to review their agreement, or they took it too lightly, and were later sued for breach of contract. After you have sent the contract back to your lawyer with your suggested changes, edits, comments, and questions, and subsequently they have sent it back to you, make sure you do a final, thorough, review before signing—never simply assume the changes have been made. Don't live to regret spending an hour or two to protect your future. Never sign a purchase and sale agreement that still contains anything that you don't completely understand and agree with—the document is legally binding once signed.

Let me guide you through some of the key areas in the minefield that is the purchase and sale agreement. These are the things that can cause you a headache if you don't get them right.

Assets

The agreement will, or should, identify the assets to be purchased, as well as the assets that are to be excluded.

Assets included

Typically, the buyer will purchase the following assets, but each sale is unique, so don't take this list as being exhaustive.

- Practice goodwill, including all records, patient charts, X-ray images, and models for all patients, patient databases, patient files, and all other information relating to the practice. They also include the slightly less tangible right to use the clinic's existing telephone number, the practice's email address(es), website, trade name, and any social media accounts.

- All leasehold improvements.

- All office furniture, equipment, computer hardware and software, hand instruments, surgical instruments, and other chattels used, unless specifically noted as excluded.

- All inventory and supplies used in connection with the operation of the practice.

Straightforward, right? Well, you would think so, but let me tell you the story of Dr. Desmond Greedy, a past client of mine—and no, that is not his real name. Dr. Greedy received a full offer for his practice, which was excellent, and most clients would have broken out the champagne to celebrate. However, my client, without my knowledge, excluded his implant equipment and materials from the equipment appraisal and supply inventory audit. He later explained to me that he felt that such equipment was not part of a family practice and felt the buyer should pay an additional amount. From the buyer's perspective, the equipment was used in the practice to achieve the stated revenues, and therefore it was integral to the sale.

It threw a $50,000 wrench into the deal and the buyer was not impressed. She felt that my client was just being greedy and at this late stage, she began doubting his integrity. When things became difficult, Dr. Greedy offered to remove the offending implant exclusion clause. Unfortunately, the buyer walked. She felt she could no longer trust the seller.

The moral of this story is that the negotiations leading up to an offer, and the subsequent purchase and sale agreement, should be abundantly clear and comprehensive, and contain zero surprises. And, of course, you should always negotiate in good faith.

Assets excluded

The following list is not exhaustive, and your sale may contain additional exclusions. These, however, are standard to most sales.

- Cash on hand or on deposit at the closing date.

- All artwork, textbooks, and personal mementos of the seller.

- All accounts receivable of the practice as at the closing date.

- All accounts payable of the practice due and owing as of the closing date.

- All liabilities, lease obligations, and shareholder loans.

If you still have leases outstanding on any equipment, you will have to ensure any lease obligations are taken care of prior to the closing date.

Allocation of purchase price (asset sale)

In the case of an asset sale, the sales proceeds must be allocated to the various types of assets. This includes equipment, leaseholds, supplies, patient charts, etc. For tax purposes this allocation is based on the fair market value of the assets.

Unfortunately, this is often contentious and results in haggling between buyer and seller. The difficulty arises from the two parties being on opposite sides of tax law. You, the buyer, will want to maximize your tax write-offs by expensing or depreciating the tangible assets, rather than the goodwill that can only be amortized over many years. The seller, on the other hand, wants the reverse of this, so that he or she can reduce income taxes by favouring an allocation of the proceeds to the goodwill rather than to the depreciable assets.

It's basically a zero-sum game. The extra tax amount saved by the buyer becomes an additional tax cost for the seller. I suggest you leave the haggling over the purchase price allocation to your dental CPA who has likely handled many similar situations.

The asset allocation, as described above, is only necessary in the event of an asset sale. If the stock of the corporation that owns the dental practice is sold, then there is no need for the allocation of assets.

Re-treatment

As we've discussed before, agreement needs to be reached on responsibility for dental work that needs to be redone post sale. Let's explore this situation in more detail and I'll give you a few options to consider when discussing this with your buyer.

Hopefully, by the time you get to this discussion the dentist has gotten to know you, carried out their due diligence, and is aware of your reputation as a dentist. They will have some idea of the level of risk they face from your patients returning for re-treatment, but little idea of the scope of re-treatments that might be necessary.

If you are not going to continue as an associate in the practice, the purchase and sale agreement should clearly state what course of action will be taken when a patient comes back to have work redone.

In essence, the choices are simple; if a patient requires additional treatment, the buyer can either perform the rework themselves and charge the seller, or have the seller complete the work free of charge.

If only it were that straightforward. If the re-treatment diagnosis is left to the buyer's discretion, there may be a tendency to charge the seller for unnecessary treatments. This could potentially cost you a lot of money.

Here are the options/clauses I promised you earlier that your lawyer might use. They can add appropriate monetary amounts and time limitations and then turn them into legalese. Once inserted into your purchase and sale agreement these will safeguard you and formalize the course of action to be taken.

- If the buyer believes it is necessary to re-do dental work at no charge to the patient, they will notify the seller. The seller is then obliged to re-treat the patient and is responsible for associated lab fees.

- If the buyer considers it necessary to re-do dental work and does not notify the seller, the seller will not be responsible to reimburse the buyer. If the buyer notifies the seller and the seller wants the buyer to perform the re-treatment, the seller will reimburse the buyer.

- The seller's responsibility for re-treatment will only apply for a set period (usually between twelve and twenty-four months from the closing date).

As there is much uncertainty about the scope of possible re-treatment, you may want to offer the buyer a reduction in the selling price in return for removal of the re-treatment clause. The amount is usually between $10,000 and $20,000. If this is agreed, the buyer has no further recourse against the seller for any re-treatments.

Accounts Receivable

If your buyer does not purchase your accounts receivable, a mechanism needs to be in place that allows your buyer to collect the practice's (pre-sale) receivables on your behalf.

Collecting the receivables yourself can be fraught with difficulties, not least of which is that you may be tempted to be a little more aggressive in your collection techniques now that the person is not your patient. If patients leave the practice because of you chasing them for money, you could find yourself in a difficult situation with your buyer. Another reason why it is best to leave collections to the new buyer is that you are probably going to be less successful in collecting receivables. The motivation to settle an old debt lessens for patients when they have to remit to a PO Box or the private residence of the departing dentist.

Your replacement, however, will be keen to maintain the patient goodwill and will more likely be successful in collecting outstanding amounts, especially if the patient wants to continue using the clinic. The agreement should stipulate the length of time the new dentist will be responsible for collecting pre-purchase receivables, and what, if anything, should be done about any remaining accounts receivable after that period. It should also specify the collection fee, which is usually between 5%-10%.

Restrictive Covenants

Buyers will want to protect the clinic's income stream, therefore, expect to see a non-compete covenant in the agreement. Your legal advisor should review this covenant and assess its enforceability. To be enforceable, the restrictions on you must be reasonable both as to length of time and geographical scope. Even if you don't own another practice, most covenants will prevent you from providing dental services through any type of arrangement, including in the capacity of an associate, partner, consultant, or shareholder.

Usually, when the seller stays as an associate in the buyer's practice it is common to have the restrictive covenant start from the last day the seller works in the clinic, not from the day the practice is sold.

Things get a little complicated when the seller has another dental clinic within the non-compete zone. As I have experienced first-hand, this can kill a sale. Dr. Split listed her practice, which enjoyed $2 million in annual revenues. It was a dream practice in terms of profitability, growth, and location. The response was overwhelming. Buyers were lining up until they discovered that Dr. Split also owned a practice just two miles away. This changed things dramatically. No one was prepared to pay a premium price when it was very likely many patients would walk up the street to see Dr. Split at her other clinic. Eventually, she did find a buyer, but not at the original asking price, and there was a clause that saw the buyer receive monetary compensation for every patient that transferred to Dr. Split's other practice, post-sale. She was de facto paying for her own clients, with little idea of what that might cost. This situation reminds me of Stephen Covey when he says in his book, The *7 Habits of Highly Effective People*, "Begin with the end in mind."

What could Dr. Split have done differently? Of course, hindsight is 20/20 but when she planned to start a second clinic, she should have thought about the potential long-term challenges inherent in having them in such close geographical proximity, should she ever decide to sell.

Non-solicitation of patients and employees

It is common to include a clause preventing the seller from soliciting patients for a five to ten-year period after the sale. Should you break this covenant, the buyer is within their rights to take legal action. If this was to happen you would very likely be made to pay damages, which can be significant, on any revenues you billed to the buyer's patients.

Similarly, many sales agreements prohibit you from soliciting employees for, say, a five-year period. In this case, the buyer will be looking for damages from you for the breach of contract.

Assignment of lease

There should be an agreement to transfer all tenant's rights under the lease to the buyer, giving the new owner a direct tenant relationship with the landlord. Bear in mind that most leases require the landlord's consent for such an assignment. As part of the assignment, the landlord should also release you from any personal guarantees.

The buyer's lender may demand that the buyer renew the lease for the duration of the loan. That is, if their loan amortization is ten years, then the lender requires certainty that the buyer can occupy that space for the ten-year period.

Vendor's representations and warranties

Representations and warranties are the most important part of the agreement. Here is a list of some of those you will be asked to provide:

1. Proof that you have title to all practice assets free and clear of any liens, claims or other encumbrances.

2. That your license to practice dentistry has never been suspended or revoked.

3. That you know of no pending court actions, lawsuits or claims against you.

4. That your practice income and expenses are materially correct.

5. That you have not engaged in any practice-billing procedures which may violate the terms of any third-party insurance contract.

6. That you are not aware of anything that exists, or is likely to arise, that would adversely affect the operation of the practice after the sale.

From the buyer's perspective, you will need them to acknowledge that any income and expense projections provided to them by you are projections only and are not a representation or warranty relating to the future income and expenses of the practice.

These warranties are critical. Let's take that last one; if you do not have this clause in the contract, a buyer could potentially take legal action against you for misrepresentation should the actual results fall short of the income projections you gave to them. This clause alone can be a landmine that could potentially result in a large claim against you if it's not included.

Assisting with the transition

It is impossible to force you to actively cooperate with promoting the practice once it is under new ownership. However, do expect some provisions in the contract that outlines what the buyer expects in terms of transitional cooperation. Typically, you will agree to:

- Sign and distribute a letter of introduction to your patients.

- Act in good faith when transferring the goodwill of the practice to the buyer.

- Be available to consult with and advise the buyer for a period of six to nine months after the sale, at no cost.

This chapter is not meant to replace the advice of experts. Never underestimate the value of seeking expert advice; there are a multitude of legal issues that can trip you up along the way. Ideally, you want a seamless transition that has no aftershocks. The purchase and sale agreement provides you with an opportunity to protect yourself and safeguard your future.

Every practice sale is different however, and each comes with its own unique challenges. In the next chapter I'll take you through the specific things you need to know, and the things to beware of in a partial sale, purchase, and sale agreement.

8

The Purchase and Sale Agreement (Partial Sale)

In chapter seven I discussed all the things that can trip you up in that sometimes-tricky purchase and sale agreement. Everything we covered in that chapter is important to almost all sales, but things can get a little more complicated if you are not selling your entire practice. What if you just want to realize some equity from your practice without giving up work altogether?

Dr. Lee started his practice ten years ago from scratch and its growth has exceeded his expectations. He should be celebrating, but success has its own headaches; he is working six days a week to keep up with demand. Recently, patients have started to complain about long wait times for an appointment. He is so busy working in the practice that he has no time to work on the practice as a business. And, more importantly, his family life is beginning to suffer.

Lee doesn't want to sell out, he still enjoys his work and has a close relationship with his patients. He knows he needs to increase the clinic's capacity but is unsure of his options and the pros and cons involved. He talks it over with a dentist friend and concludes that bringing on a like-minded associate, who would eventually become his business partner, would be the best answer to sharing the workload, expanding the practice, and planning for retirement. He sees the incoming dentist purchasing a one-half share of the practice initially, and later purchasing the remaining half.

Sounds perfect, doesn't it? Dr. Lee would be able to spend more time with his family, put some money away toward retirement, maintain his current cash flow, and as a bonus perhaps work less hours. It could be perfect; that is, if he can avoid all the pitfalls along the way. Lee is considering two popular group practice models, the "Solo Group" arrangement and the "Partnership" model. Both have their pros and cons, and both have potential hazards to avoid.

The Solo Group Model

This structure leads to there being two independent practices operating under the same roof. It is popular with dentists who want to be their own boss, and yet get the benefit of sharing costs with another dentist. In a cost-share arrangement, the funding of the day-to-day operation of the practice is summarized in a cost-sharing agreement. The parties can also choose to enter into a separate buy-sell agreement to deal with unforeseen events such as death, disability, or the dentist leaving the clinic, which I will discuss later.

Finding the perfect partner

This is one of those hazards I was talking about—great partner, happy life, bad partner, trouble and strife. I'm sure you know or have heard of dentists in dysfunctional co-ownership arrangements. They are usually vocal, and you can recognize them by their haggard looks, the bags under their eyes, and the way they clench their jaws whenever they talk about their partner. Overheard at a cocktail party or business event, they will be the people saying something like, "My partner in my practice and I lead separate lives, it's like we are in two different practices—we barely speak." Or maybe, "She's always first out of the door at night, leaving me to close up shop. And, of course, it's me that has to manage the practice."

Conflicts like this arise because the principal dentist failed to determine if the dentist they brought on board was partnership material. If you want to avoid this catastrophic mistake, don't be so desperate that you accept the first person that possesses a dental degree and has the cheque in hand. You don't want to solve one problem and create a dozen new ones. You need to ask the right questions, do a ton of due diligence, and get to know the person beyond a twenty-minute "on best behavior" interview.

Getting it wrong can lead to serious problems. It's difficult to dismantle a relationship that has gone sour after an associate has worked in your clinic for several years and built up a sizable clientele. I've come across dentists who were procrastinating about finalizing the sale with an associate because they were having doubts about the dentist with whom they had chosen to be partners. Unfortunately, when that happens there will come a stage when the associate will begin to pressure you to complete the sale and consummate your relationship. If you bring onboard the wrong person and don't realize or face up to the situation early in the relationship you could find yourself in an impossible situation. At some point, your associate may threaten to leave the practice if you delay the sale. Now you are in a Catch-22 situation—you can either go through with the sale or find a new partner—neither choice is good for business or your stress levels. If you choose the first option, your new partner is unlikely to change their behavior. They will not magically turn over a new leaf and start working later and help manage the practice.

Choosing the right associate and person with whom to partner is therefore vital. Ask your staff to prepare a profile of who they would see as the ideal candidate. They often have a deeper, more objective insight into the attributes a new dentist will need to succeed in the practice.

Initial associateship

Even after doing your due diligence, it is still important to have the new dentist join the practice as an associate before you sell them a share. Working together in the practice will let you and your staff assess their compatibility and whether they are going to be beneficial to the practice. Are they, as you hoped when you interviewed them, partnership material? Are they going to pull their weight?

The associate period is usually about two years, or when they achieve pre-agreed revenue targets. This is important, as reaching these targets indicates that they will be able to meet their financial obligations regarding practice overhead, and at the same time cover their living expenses. The one caveat to this is to cut your losses as early as possible if you realize within a few months that you have chosen the wrong candidate.

There are several ways you can set the date the associate will purchase their share of the practice. For example, you can agree on a fixed date, or peg the purchase date to when the associate reaches pre-agreed revenue thresholds. Always build into any agreement a three- to six-month trial period, during which either party can walk away. As I mentioned earlier, avoid inaction if things are not going well. Monitor your relationship, and how they work, carefully in those early months. Things to watch out for include: their relationship with staff, their professionalism, leadership skills, energy, commitment, how they relate to patients, and the quality of their dentistry. If you are going to pull the plug, pull it as early as possible. Once the trial period ends, the new dentist must make a financial commitment to move the sale ahead and close the deal. Obtain a good-faith deposit, usually after a short (maybe three-month) trial period. A new dentist's professed commitment to the practice means nothing unless it is backed by cash. Once the initial three- to six-month trial period is over and both parties agree to move forward, you should expect the new dentist to make a sizable, refundable deposit. If finance is a challenge for the associate, the deposit can take the form of sweat equity. For instance, an agreed amount could be withheld from the associate's monthly remuneration and held in trust by the practice.

How should the purchase price be established?

This is tricky. On the one hand it might appear that the best course of action is to value the practice once the associate has spent a few years building their patient list. The problem you face is that the associate will see this as punishing their performance. The more revenue they bring in, the more the practice is worth, and the more they will have to pay. This is a baked-in performance disincentive. Two years in and you may have a disillusioned associate who leaves the practice for a better ownership opportunity elsewhere. So, how do you establish a fair purchase price for the associate? There are many ways to approach this challenge. Here is one example that I have seen be effective.

The practice is valued at the beginning of the associateship. For this example, let's assume the total practice value is $800,000, with $600,000 attributable to goodwill and $200,000 for tangible assets, equipment, etc. Two years later, at the time of purchase, a new valuation is carried out and the practice value has increased by $400,000 to $1.2 million. This is all attributable to an increase in goodwill that is the result of increased patient flow. For argument's sake, let's assume both dentists treated approximately the same number of new patients over that period.

If we take the new valuation, the associate—if they are buying half of the practice—would be on the hook for $600,000. My suggestion is that the associate receives a 50% discount on the $400,000 increase to the value of the practice. In our example above, this would result in a purchase price of $500,000. This takes into account the fact that the associate was responsible for half of the increase in value of the practice.

The cost-sharing arrangement

Once the sale is complete you will continue to receive all the revenue you generate, as does your new cost-share partner. However, post-sale you both contribute to overhead using a cost-sharing formula. Here is one example of how costs might be allocated:

- Dental supplies are split in proportion to the monthly revenue of each dentist.

- Individual practice expenses (e.g., laboratory fees, salaries for staff who work exclusively for one dentist, and professional expenses such as licences and insurance).

- All remaining practice expenses are shared equally, (e.g., salaries for common staff, rent, advertising and promotion, and general office expenses).

The benefit to you of cost-sharing is that it increases your take-home pay. It is important to recognize the significant benefits of cost-sharing within a group arrangement. In some cases, dentists hardly communicate and stop sharing staff, supplies, and equipment. What a lost opportunity.

In addition to allocating costs, the cost-share agreement also deals with patient allocation. There is often a clause that states that new patients are allocated to whichever dentist has the first available appointment, which means that most land with the new dentist. An alternative clause might state that new patients are shared equally.

The buy-sell arrangement

The buy-sell arrangement, which deals with retirement, disability, death, and malpractice, is crucial in a group practice to provide an orderly exit. This is important; its provisions will preserve the equity both parties have accumulated in the practice. These provisions are not required in a cost-share arrangement, but many dentists think they are essential to protect the value of their investment. Here are a few examples which might trigger a buy-out.

Mandatory withdrawal

In the case of one partner receiving a licence suspension or acting in a manner that results in the practice suffering an unacceptable hit to its reputation in the dental community, the departing dentist will be required to sell the practice to the other dentist. The purchase price will be discounted by 50 percent, based on a fair-market valuation, and must be paid within 60 days.

Buy/sell on death

In case of the death of the cost-share partner, the purchase price of the practice must be paid in full by the remaining dentist in equal monthly instalments, no later than six months after the date of death. Life insurance policies can be taken out that will cover the buyout costs.

Buy/sell and long-term disability

If a dentist becomes disabled for more than a year, the remaining dentist is required to purchase the disabled dentist's practice at a 10% discount based on practice valuation, to be paid in monthly installments over six months. The parties may arrange for a disability buy-out policy. However, most practitioners don't do this because the policies can be prohibitively expensive

The right of first refusal

A standard clause in these types of agreement is the right of first refusal. It states that no dentist shall sell or transfer their practice to another dentist unless they have first offered to sell to his or her partner. While it may seem a common courtesy to offer the practice to the cost-sharing partner, this clause can be a deal killer, as shown in the scenario below.

For the past ten years, a sixty-five-year-old dentist, Dr. Senior, has had a cost-share arrangement with a forty-five-year-old dentist, Dr. Junior. The younger dentist is keen to renovate the clinic and update the equipment at considerable expense. Dr. Senior is considering retiring within a few years, so he views the expense very differently to his younger partner. Since his partner does not want to contribute to the cost, Dr. Junior is obviously reluctant to commit to a large capital expenditure unless he owns the whole clinic.

Naturally, this leads Dr. Senior to consider selling his share of the practice to his partner. After several meetings, Dr. Junior offers $500,000. Dr. Senior does not accept. The relationship, understandably, becomes strained. Unable to reach an agreement, Dr. Senior puts his share of the practice on the market and receives a cash offer of $800,000. Obviously, he is ecstatic. A little later in the day, he decides to review his cost-share agreement only to discover the first-refusal clause that states he must present the offer to his partner, who has 30 days to decide whether to purchase Dr. Senior's share of the practice on the same terms and conditions as the offer he has in hand. If not, he must allow the third-party offer to proceed.

Unfortunately for Dr. Senior, the agreement has an unusual requirement whereby the prospective third-party buyer is required to disclose his financial assets as proof that he has sufficient financial assets to make the purchase. This was added to the agreement by one of their lawyers to prevent either party from soliciting less than genuine offers that would pressure the remaining party to increase the amount they would have to pay.

In this situation, Dr. Senior has already anticipated that his partner is going to be difficult, and he knows that his partner has had preliminary talks with his lawyer. He is forcing Dr. Junior to either pay more than he wants to, to own the entire practice, or accept a partner he doesn't even know. Within days, the $800,000 offer was withdrawn. The prospective buyer could see that his offer was being used as a negotiating tool to extract more money from the seller's partner and felt the thirty-day wait period was unreasonable. He felt insulted that his ability to pay was being questioned, and that it was an invasion of his privacy that the seller was demanding that he reveal his net worth. You can't blame him for walking away.

I don't mean to frighten you from having a first refusal clause in your purchase and sale agreement altogether; you just have to be a little careful with the wording. This clause can still be valuable, as it gives the remaining dentist an opportunity to purchase the practice rather than have a partner thrust upon them. The key to making it work in your favor as the senior partner is to see things from a prospective purchasers' perspective and make things a little more convenient. Cut the traditional thirty-day decision period to seven days, and don't force the prospect to disclose their finances—this has no place in a buy-sell agreement. Your partner knows the practice intimately, so they should be able to decide whether they want to purchase your share within that time. This is especially true given that you would have had at least some provisional discussions prior to the time clause being enacted.

The scenario above is not uncommon. I have been asked by clients many times, "If I am not able to sell my practice, will I be forced to accept a token offer from my partner?"

My suggestion to clients is to have a mandatory retirement clause. This will insure you are able to cash in your investment in the clinic for a reasonable price.

The Mandatory Retirement Clause

The most likely reason a senior dentist withdraws from their practice is to retire, so I am always amazed that buy-sell agreements rarely address the looming issue of retirement. I always advise clients to add a withdrawal clause guaranteeing a retirement buyout in case a successor can't be found. Without it you can run into a sticky situation, as was explained to me by a dentist at a conference. I'll let Kristy, a sixty-six-year-old dentist, tell you the story.

"I was planning on retiring and approached my junior partner, Brad, and asked him if he wanted to buy me out. He wasn't keen. He reminded me that he already had a large patient base and didn't want to take on any more work. I understood where he was coming from and put my half of the practice up for sale. I was feeling good, I'd done the right thing; Brad wasn't keen, so I took steps to move on with my life. Then things got difficult. Although I got a lot of interest from prospective buyers for my half of the practice, every time I brought an interested party into the clinic Brad was, well, a brat. He was surly, curt, uncommunicative to the point of being rude. It was obvious to everyone he was not going to accept a new partner easily. Not surprisingly, my prospects quickly disappeared. I was at a loss as to how to handle the situation. There was simply no way forward."

Kristy was counting on the money from the sale to provide her with a comfortable retirement lifestyle. Unfortunately, she couldn't spend any more time in such a poisonous relationship, so she decided to leave the clinic without a penny after she had spent her career building a successful practice.

Not being able to sell the clinic, Brad ended up taking over Kristy's practice. She was devastated. Brad, of course, laughed all the way to the bank when he later sold the senior dentist's half to another dentist. I will never forget this incident, which is why I always advise clients to put in a mandatory retirement clause. There can be various wordings, but in essence it states that should you try and fail to sell your share of the practice, you give you cost-share partner 180-days' notice that they are obliged to buy you out. To make this a little more palatable, there is usually a discount involved of, say, 20% less than the appraised value.

The Partnership Model

In this model, things start out in a similar way to the solo group option; a busy dentist in a growing practice is looking to cash out on their equity. If the practice is a corporate entity, instead of selling one-half of the practice's assets, the purchasing dentist will be required to purchase the stock of the corporation. There are significant tax differences between buying assets versus stock, and you will need to rely on your CPA to guide you in your specific situation.

It's also possible that two partners may decide to have a partnership with two separate corporations. Under this arrangement, a management company is usually set up to manage the clinic, track the revenues, and pay the expenses.

The essence of a partnership is the sharing of profits, regardless of who generates the income. In my experience, it's not in dentists' DNA to share profits based on ownership; they are raised on the "eat-what-you-kill" principle. Hence, the partnership often provides for each partner to receive income based on the revenues produced by the partner.

An advantage of a having a partnership is that it is easy to add new partners by selling a share of the partnership. A possible disadvantage, however, is that as a partner you have obligations to the partnership which you are obliged to fulfill. This includes taking responsibility for the management of the practice. These obligations will almost certainly include committing to a minimum number of hours working in the clinic, and the possibility of incurring financial penalties should you decide to quit the partnership.

Despite this, partnerships are growing. Having partners to absorb some of the workload and share the burden of management will allow you to achieve a greater work-life balance. Having partners to look after your patients when you need time off is a blessing, especially if you bring onboard partners that you can trust and who pull their weight.

Selling Your Practice for the Most Money Checklist

Okay, you've thought long and hard about selling your practice, and have read everything I've had to say about the subject. You've taken into consideration all the pros and cons, and now you are chomping at the bit to get on with the sale. Hold on there! Not just yet. This book has focused on helping you maximize your return on investment, and you can't do that if you rush into things. Dentists who wake up one morning and say to themselves, or their significant other, "I'm going to call a broker and sell the clinic," and then do just that, not only leave a ton of money on the table, but transitioning the practice almost kills them. I exaggerate not—there is so much that can go wrong, so many pitfalls, and so many ways you can ruin lives (including your own). And don't get me started on the damage you could potentially do to your reputation.

Planning is everything. I love this quote from J.R.R. Tolkien's *The Hobbit*, "It does not do to leave a live dragon out of your calculations, if you live near one." Take it from me, there are fire-breathing dragons all around you when it comes to selling your practice. Like Bilbo Baggins, Tolkien's Hobbit, you are on a quest to win treasure—the "gold" you have spent years accumulating in your practice. I'm talking about equipment, systems, trained staff, patients, and goodwill. If you are to maximize this "treasure," you will need to make your practice look wildly attractive to suitors well in advance of them turning up on your doorstep.

Before you do anything, however, you should strategize the sale. Remember, it's never too early to start. As the Chinese proverb says, "The best time to plant a tree was 20 years ago. The second-best time is now."

If you want to sell your practice for more than you ever imagined, it's easy, just focus on the following eleven transition planning points, and then use the checklist that follows to keep you on track.

1. Focus on boosting your practice value by improving revenues.

2. Assemble a professional transition team.

3. Ensure you will have enough money after the sale to lead the life you want to live, for the rest of your life.

4. Know when you are truly ready to sell.

5. Don't focus solely on money.

6. Choose the right person to whom you will sell.

7. Build a strong team in advance.

8. Connect with the buyer, but don't negotiate with them.

9. Put yourself in the buyer's shoes.

10. Give your clinic a facelift.

11. Minimize your post-sale obligations.

With the above points in mind, here is a checklist of the key things you need to do to sell your practice for the best possible price:

☐ Improve the conversion rate of phone inquiries into appointments.

☐ Increase the number of active patients who are scheduled for their next appointment.

☐ Reduce the practice's patient attrition rate.

☐ Reactivate your inactive patient base.

☐ Hire an office manager whose responsibility it is to ensure you are meeting your practice revenue targets.

☐ Retain a CPA experienced in working with dental practices.

☐ Retain a lawyer who works with dental practices.

☐ Bring onboard a quarterback (i.e., a transition specialist or broker).

☐ Do the numbers; discover how much money you really need to retire comfortably.

☐ Talk to your financial planner and your CPA about setting up a worry-free retirement portfolio.

☐ Take the Purtzki mirror test. When you first look at yourself in the mirror each morning ask yourself, "If I had only a few days left on this earth, would I go to my practice today?" If, for five mornings in a row you answer in the negative, you are ready to transition into retirement without looking back with regret.

☐ Think about your legacy and your reputation. You worked hard to build a thriving career on your integrity. For a few more dollars, don't let a stranger destroy it.

☐ Sell to a compatible person whose values you share, and who aligns with your practice philosophy.

☐ Have a buy/sell agreement to ensure you get a fair value for your practice when you leave.

☐ Ensure your team is a strong asset in the sale of your practice. If necessary, "clean house" well in advance of looking for a purchaser.

☐ Build a trusting relationship with the prospective buyer, without getting involved directly with the negotiations.

☐ Don't be greedy. Leave some juice on the table for the buyer, it will benefit you in the long run.

☐ If your clinic is a little worn, consider enhancing its "curb appeal" by investing in a facelift. Hip practices sell for more.

☐ Consult with your lawyer before finalizing the purchase and sale agreement. Ask yourself:

 ☐ Is there a listing of dental equipment, furnishings, and other equipment?

 ☐ Is there a list of assets that are excluded from the purchase?

 ☐ Does the purchase price allocation help me to minimize the tax liability?

 ☐ If patients need re-treatment, do I have the option to either do the work without charge, or negotiate a discounted fee if the buyer does the rework?

 ☐ Is the amount and period of time for any rework restricted?

 ☐ Have we outlined how accounts receivable are dealt with?

☐ Are accounts receivable part of the purchase price?

☐ Does the agreement require the buyer to collect the receivables and remit to me promptly?

☐ Have we negotiated a lower fee with the buyer for collecting the receivables?

☐ Did we pay any outstanding credit balances to patients?

☐ Did we ensure that there is only a minimum restrictive covenant in place, both as to geographical scope and duration?

☐ Did we obtain confirmation on the lease assignment that states that I am no longer responsible in any way for the lease?

☐ What is the post-closing financial and legal exposure for my "statements and warranties" in the agreement?

☐ Schedule an appointment with a transition expert to make sure your transaction is stress free and structured to allow the maximum financial benefit for your retirement.

One last thing: once it's over, don't look back!

A

Acknowledgements

First, I'd like to thank Mike Wicks, my collaborator on this book. He helped me find my voice and made the book both readable and accessible. His commitment and passion for the book were motivating. He helped make the whole process enjoyable and a lot easier than I ever thought possible.

A special thank you to Dr. Fern Savoie, who was instrumental in launching my dental specialty career. He was also my first dentist client when I founded my CPA firm in 1980. Being well respected in the dental community, he referred me to many of his colleagues over the years.

My heartfelt thanks go out to the following very successful dentists for taking time out of their busy schedules to read and comment on the manuscript. Your comments and suggestions were invaluable. I am honored and flattered by the endorsements they gave The Simple Guide to Selling Your Dental Practice for More Money. Thank you: Dr. Ivan Kahn; Dr. Ron G. Smith; Dr. Dean Nomura; Dr. Jehan Casey.

Thank you to the Blue Beetle Books publishing team. Paul Abra for handling production and promotion, Tom Spetter for designing such an amazing jacket and for laying the book out with such style, Kara Anderson for her considerable copyediting skills, Sheila Wicks for proofreading the final manuscript to ensure there were no embarrassing typos, and finally Mike Wicks for his ongoing publishing guidance.

Finally, I want to thank my wife Marie for her encouragement and unconditional support. Without her, I would never have been able to write this book.

Notes:

Notes:

Notes:

Notes:

Notes:

www.ingramcontent.com/pod-product-compliance
Lightning Source LLC
Chambersburg PA
CBHW071722210326
41597CB00017B/2560